Open Before Christmas

Devotional Thoughts for the Holiday Season

From Will Vaus

Open Before Christmas
Devotional Thoughts for the Holiday Season

Copyright © 2012 Will Vaus

Barnabas Books
a division of Winged Lion Press
Hamden, CT

All rights reserved. Except in the case of quotations embodied in critical articles or reviews, no part of this book may be reproduced or transmitted in any form or by any means, electronic or mechanical, including photocopying, recording, or by any information storage or retrieval system, without written permission of the publisher.
For information, contact Winged Lion Press www.WingedLionPress.com

Unless otherwise noted Scripture references are taken from the HOLY BIBLE, NEW INTERNATIONAL VERSION ®. Copyright © 1973, 1978, 1984 International Bible Society.
Used by permission of Zondervan. All rights reserved.

Winged Lion Press titles may be purchased for business or promotional use or special sales.

10-9-8-7-6-5-4-3-2-1

ISBN-13 978-1-935688-006

This book is dedicated to
my brothers
Dennis, Steve & Roger
with whom I share
many treasured memories
of Christmases past.

Table of Contents

Introduction	1
The First Sunday of Advent	6
Monday of the First Week	9
Tuesday of the First Week	11
Wednesday of the First Week	14
Thursday of the First Week	17
Friday of the First Week	20
Saturday of the First Week	23
The Second Sunday of Advent	27
Monday of the Second Week	30
Tuesday of the Second Week	34
Wednesday of the Second Week	37
Thursday of the Second Week	40
Friday of the Second Week	43
Saturday of the Second Week	46
The Third Sunday of Advent	48
Monday of the Third Week	50
Tuesday of the Third Week	52
Wednesday of the Third Week	54
Thursday of the Third Week	57
Friday of the Third Week	60
Saturday of the Third Week	62

The Fourth Sunday of Advent	66
Monday of the Fourth Week	68
Tuesday of the Fourth Week	70
Wednesday of the Fourth Week	72
Thursday of the Fourth Week	75
Friday of the Fourth Week	77
Christmas Eve	80
Christmas Day	83
The Second Day of Christmas	85
The Third Day of Christmas	87
The Fourth Day of Christmas	89
The Fifth Day of Christmas	92
The Sixth Day of Christmas	94
The Seventh Day of Christmas	96
The Eighth Day of Christmas	98
The Ninth Day of Christmas	101
The Tenth Day of Christmas	103
The Eleventh Day of Christmas	106
The Twelfth Day of Christmas	108
Epiphany	110
Conclusion	112
End Notes	115

INTRODUCTION

As a child, I recall that waiting for Christmas Day to arrive was a very difficult thing. I remember a special Advent Calendar my parents bought for me when I was very young. The mere sight of that calendar filled my mind with the hope of magical happenings just around the corner. Each day the sense of suspense would build as I would open a new door on that calendar and see a picture of something or someone related to the Christmas story—only 24 more days until Christmas, then 23, 22, 21....

Of course, what I was most looking forward to, as a child, was opening my presents on Christmas morning. Even that experience was shrouded with an intriguing ritual created by my parents. Sleeping through the night on Christmas Eve was, naturally, nigh to impossible. Finally, in the early hours of Christmas morning I would creep out of my bedroom at the end of the hall and join my brothers at the top of the stairs. We would listen intently to my parents' movements down below, but we knew the unwritten rule: "No coming downstairs until you hear the music."

The music we listened for, ever so carefully, were the strains of "Rudolf the Red-Nosed Reindeer" sung by the Bison Glee Club. (I still have the record and play it for my children on Christmas morning, so the tradition carries on.) Once we heard the music, we knew it was safe to come downstairs and open those long-awaited gifts.

I'm sure every child can identify with the difficulty of obeying the instructions neatly printed on many a Christmas present: "Don't Open Until December 25". The desire to "just take a peak" ahead of time, or at least shake a gift or two, is almost irresistible. However, I was a rather compliant boy and so the closest I ever came to opening a present before December 25 was simply to touch the glittering wrapping on a box or two, or three.

You might wonder where Jesus was in our family celebration of Christmas. He was there to be sure. We attended worship services at our local church, Sunday by Sunday. I even remember one Christmas, when I was a very little boy, my father dressed up as Santa Claus for a church Christmas party, not that I knew the real identity of that particular Santa at the time. That event sums up, in a way, the approach to Christmas taken by my parents during the days of my childhood and youth. There was a delightful mixture of what some might call the "pagan" elements of the holiday and the more serious Christian meaning. I know that some Christian parents today worry about such a mixture misleading their children and so they banish Santa, Rudolf and all the rest from their celebration of Christmas. While I can understand those concerns, I don't really share them. I guess that is because I know from my own experience, that the hovering presence of Santa every December never kept me from learning what the holiday was really all about and coming to worship Jesus at the center of it all. I believe C. S. Lewis has written very helpfully on this issue....

> There is a stage in a child's life at which it cannot separate the religious from the merely festal character of Christmas or Easter. I have been told of a very small and very devout boy who was heard murmuring to himself on Easter morning a poem of his own composition which began "Chocolate eggs and Jesus risen". This seems to me, for his age, both admirable poetry and admirable piety. But of course the time will soon come when such a child can no longer effortlessly and spontaneously enjoy that unity. He will become able to distinguish the spiritual from the ritual and festal aspect of Easter; chocolate eggs will no longer be sacramental. And once he has distinguished he must put one or the other first. If he puts the spiritual first he can still taste something of Easter in the chocolate eggs; if he puts the eggs first they will soon be no more than any other sweetmeat. They have taken on an independent, and therefore a soon withering, life.[1]

For my own part, I believe I can still taste Easter in chocolate eggs and savor Christmas in eggnog.

It wasn't until my teen years that I learned there was more to Advent than opening the doors of a colorful calendar. During my youth, I was an active member in a local church that routinely celebrated Advent with the lighting of Advent candles in worship, the publication of an Advent devotional booklet each year, and an Advent craft workshop at the beginning of December for families with young children. Every Christmas Eve our church would host a Christmas pageant in which all ages participated, and every year I played a different character in the Christmas story. One year I was a shepherd; another time my brothers and I portrayed the three wise men (wise guys would have been more like it). However, my greatest role of all was as the angel Gabriel. I was over six feet in height by that time and I was privileged to wear sparkling white wings that were almost as wide as I was tall. The church traditions surrounding Advent and Christmas during my youth certainly deepened my delight in both the festal and the more sincerely religious aspects of the season.

However, it wasn't until I became a pastor myself that the joy of the Advent season found a permanent place in my heart. I think I can truly say it is my favorite time of year to be a preacher. The themes of Advent and Christmas, while so familiar to many, never lose their magic for me, and we can never adequately explore their depths. Thus, for many years, I have made it a habit to preach, as many pastors do throughout this season, on the themes and Scriptures that tell the Christmas story, from the First Sunday of Advent all the way through to Epiphany on January 6.

As I have preached through the Advent and Christmas seasons for many a year now, I have also learned more about the traditions and the history of this season in the Church Year. The word "advent" comes from the Latin "adventus" and means "arrival" or "coming". Thus, the season is one of preparation and expectant waiting for the arrival of Christ: a remembrance of his first coming as a babe in Bethlehem, and a glorious looking forward to his second coming when he will judge the world and establish his eternal kingdom.

The origin of the celebration of Advent in the Western Church goes back at least as early as the fourth century after Christ. A feast day celebrating the birth of Jesus was established in the latter part of that century. Some churches originally celebrated the Feast of the Nativity on December 25, others on January 6, the latter date becoming for the Western Church the Feast of Epiphany. There are Christian sermons dating from the fifth and sixth centuries that talk about preparing for the Feast of the Nativity. However, these sermons do not mention an official season of Advent. A church synod held in AD 581 established that Mondays, Wednesdays, and Fridays from November 11 until the Feast of the Nativity, Mass should be celebrated according to the rite for Lent. Thus, the season of Advent was originally more penitential in character. A collection of sermons from St Gregory the Great (whose papacy was from 590 to 604) included a sermon for the Second Sunday of Advent, and by AD 650, five Advent Sundays were being celebrated in Spain. It was Gregory VII, pope from 1073 to 1085, who reduced the number of Advent Sundays to four.[2]

Traditionally, the color associated with Advent is purple, symbolizing the royalty of Christ the King as well as being the color associated with penance. Some churches now use the color blue (also a color of royalty) to distinguish the Advent season from that of Lent and to focus more on the hope of Christ.

The beginning of Advent is often a time for "the hanging of the greens" in various churches with green being an appropriate symbol of everlasting life and growth in Christ. This practice finds its origin in the life of the pre-Christian Germanic peoples who, in the cold and darkness of December in

Northern Europe, would bring greens into their homes and light fires as signs of hope for the coming of spring. Christians eventually adopted some of these pagan traditions, using them instead to celebrate their hope in Christ. By the sixteenth century, both Catholics and Protestants in Germany were using greens and candles in their celebration of Advent. From there, these practices spread throughout Christendom.[3]

At the center of the hanging of the greens is the Advent Wreath that, in its circular form, commemorates the eternity of God. In the midst of the wreath are four candles, three purple (or blue) and one pink. Each Sunday in Advent a candle is lit, symbolizing the coming of the light of God into our world. The pink candle is often lit on the Third Sunday, which is traditionally associated with the theme of joy. The other Sundays also have various themes commonly connected with them such as hope, love and peace. At the center of the Advent Wreath is a white candle, symbolizing the purity of Christ. It is usually lit on Christmas Eve or Christmas Day.[4]

Various Scripture readings have been associated with Advent for hundreds of years, following the lectionaries of different churches. The devotional thoughts contained in this book do not follow all of the Advent readings of the Revised Common Lectionary followed by Catholic and many Protestant churches. However, many of the Scriptures traditionally associated with Advent and Christmas are, rather fully, explored herein.

For many years, the song *The Twelve Days of Christmas* was my only source of information for this particular season in the Church Year. I, like many people, did not even know when the twelve days began and ended. Nor could I tell you the origin of this celebration. However, the Catholic Encyclopedia indicates that the origin of the celebration of The Twelve Days goes back at least to The Council of Tours that established, in 566 or 567, the sanctity of the twelve days from Christmas to Epiphany, the latter holiday being the day in the Western Church calendar when the arrival of the Magi is celebrated.[5]

This book is designed for use as a personal devotional tool beginning with the First Sunday of Advent and following through to Epiphany. It is also created without dates so that it may be used more than once if the reader so desires. The idea is to read one selection per day throughout the Advent and Christmas seasons.

Advent begins on the fourth Sunday before Christmas Day, which is the Sunday nearest to November 30. Enough selections are included in this book so that it may be used in years when the First Sunday of Advent falls on the earliest possible date: November 27.

Now you have in hand a present you can open before Christmas, and keep on opening right through to Epiphany. May God bless you as you remember and celebrate the first coming of Christ and as you look forward to and prepare

Devotional Thoughts for the Holiday Season

for his second coming.

THE FIRST SUNDAY OF ADVENT

After telling a class of four to seven year olds the story of Adam and Eve, a Sunday school teacher began to quiz them. "What was Eve's punishment for disobeying God?" she asked her class.

A bright-eyed girl raised her hand and said: "She had to crawl on her belly and eat dirt for the rest of her life."[6]

Actually, according to Genesis, crawling on one's belly and eating dirt was part of the curse that was placed upon the serpent. We read the rest of the curse and what I call the "announcement of Christmas in paradise" in Genesis 3:15. The Lord God said to the serpent...

> And I will put enmity
> > between you and the woman,
> > and between your offspring and hers;
> he will crush your head,
> > and you will strike his heel.

I believe this verse foretells three things about Christ who was to come. First, it foretells Christ's incarnation.

The offspring of the woman is the Lord Jesus Christ. The word *offspring* in Genesis 3:15 is sometimes translated as *seed* or *seed of the woman*. It is unique in the Bible. Genesis 3:15 is the only place where the phrase, *seed of the woman*, appears in all of Scripture.

The word *seed*, as used in Genesis 3:15, refers to a man's semen. Clearly, a woman does not have seed. So what did God mean when he said to the serpent: "I will put enmity between you and the woman, and between your seed and hers."?

The manner in which God's curse upon the serpent was traditionally understood was that there would be hatred between our first parents and the serpent and between all of their *posterity* and the serpent's *posterity*. The oldest Jewish interpretation, found in the third century B.C., took the serpent as symbolic of Satan. The Jews looked for a victory over Satan to come in the days of the Messiah. Christians later understood the serpent of Genesis 3 in the same way. That is why Revelation 20:2 refers to "that ancient serpent, who is the devil, or Satan." Therefore, by the serpent's seed we are to understand the devil and all his children, who are permitted by God to tempt his people.

As early as the second century A.D., some of the Early Church Fathers, such as Justin Martyr and Irenaeus of Lyons, regarded Genesis 3:15 as the Protoevangelium, the first announcement of the Good News, the first messianic prophecy in the Hebrew Scriptures. Genesis 3:15 was also regarded as the first prophecy of the virgin birth because it is the only place in the Bible that speaks of "the seed of the woman". Since a woman doesn't have seed, someone else must supply it. That seed was supplied to one woman in an unusual way. That woman was Mary, who twice in the Gospel of John (2:4 and 19:26) is referred to by Jesus as "woman." Jesus himself is the seed of that woman.

I said that the phrase *the seed of the woman* appears only once in the Bible. That is true. However, there is a similar verse. It is in Revelation 12:17 where we read, "Then the dragon was enraged at the woman and went off to make war against the rest of her offspring—those who obey God's commandments and hold to the testimony of Jesus." Here I believe the *woman* is definitely Mary, who at the beginning of Revelation 12 gives birth to Jesus. Notice in this chapter that it says the dragon, that is symbolic of Satan, makes war against her children, that is, the followers of Jesus. The thing to notice is that the Greek word for seed, *spermatos*, is used in this verse. Again, it speaks of a woman's seed. In light of Revelation 12:17 it becomes clear why the Early Church understood Genesis 3:15 to be the first proclamation of the virgin birth of Jesus.

How did God supply the seed for Mary to conceive Jesus? We don't know exactly how God did it, other than the fact that he did *not* do it in the normal way, by a man having sexual relations with a woman. The angel simply says to Mary, "The Holy Spirit will come upon you, and the power of the Most High will overshadow you. So the holy one to be born will be called the Son of God." (Luke 1:35)

This miracle speaks great encouragement to us. We have a Savior who is bone of our bone and flesh of our flesh. Hebrews 2:11 and 14 say, "Both the one who makes men holy and those who are made holy are of the same family. So Jesus is not ashamed to call them brothers.... Since the children have flesh and blood, he too shared in their humanity..." How amazing, that God would stoop to take on our flesh and blood, to share in our humanity.

Joe Torre had been a catcher and a broadcast announcer for the St. Louis Cardinals. Shortly after he was named manager, according to the *Pittsburgh Press*, New York Yankees' announcer Phil Rizzuto suggested that managing could be done better from high above the baseball field—from the level of the broadcasting booth.

Torre replied, "Upstairs, you can't look in their eyes."

In Jesus Christ, the seed of the woman, God chose to come down on the field and look into our eyes.

MONDAY OF THE FIRST WEEK

> "And I will put enmity
>   between you and the woman,
>   and between your offspring and hers;
>   he will crush your head,
>   and you will strike his heel."

A second thing that Genesis 3:15 foretells is Christ's suffering and death. This is indicated in the serpent's bruising his heel, which has traditionally been interpreted as a reference to Christ's human nature. Satan bruised Christ's heel when he tempted him for forty days in the wilderness. He bruised his heel when he raised strong persecution against him during the time of his public ministry. Satan, in a special manner, bruised Christ's heel when our Lord complained that his soul was exceedingly sorrowful, even unto death, and he sweat great drops of blood, falling to the ground, in the Garden of Gethsemane. Satan bruised Christ's heel when he put it into the heart of Judas to betray Christ. Satan bruised Christ yet most of all, when Jesus was nailed to the cross, and he cried out, "My God, my God, why have you forsaken me?"

This is the reason why the Son of God became human. He was born expressly that he might die for our sin, paying our penalty, so that we could be reunited to God, restored to paradise. How amazing, not only that God would become human, but that he would identify with our suffering, that he, the Creator of the Universe, would allow part of his creation, Satan, to bruise his glorious heel.

Joseph Damien was a nineteenth-century missionary who ministered to people with leprosy on the island of Molokai, Hawaii. Those suffering from leprosy grew to love him and revered the sacrificial life he lived out before them.

One morning before Damien was to lead daily worship, he was pouring some hot water into a cup when the water swirled out and fell on to his bare foot. It took him a moment to realize that he had not felt any sensation. Gripped by the sudden fear of what this could mean, he poured more hot water on the same spot. He had no feeling whatsoever.

Damien immediately knew what had happened. As he walked tearfully to deliver his sermon, no one at first noticed the difference in his opening line. He normally began every sermon with, "My fellow believers." However, this morning he began with, "My fellow lepers."[7]

In an even greater way, Jesus came into this world knowing what it would cost. He bore in his pure being the marks of evil so that we might be made pure. He allowed the serpent to bruise his heal, so that by his stripes we might be healed. (Isaiah 53:5)

Sir Thomas Browne once said, "For death is the cure of all diseases." Truly, Christ's death was the cure for all diseases, especially the disease of sin.

An article in *National Geographic* (September 1991) tells of a young man from Hanover, Pennsylvania, who was badly burned in a boiler explosion. To save his life, physicians covered him with six thousand centimeters of donor skin, as well as sheets of skin cultured from a stamp-sized piece of his own unburned flesh.

A journalist asked him, "Do you ever think about the donor who saved you?"

The young man replied, "To be alive because of a dead donor is too big, too much, so I don't think about it."

Christians have received a similar gift—overwhelming, and worth thinking about. The Son of God became human so that he could give his life for us, his pure flesh to cover all the places where our skin was burned with sin. As we celebrate Advent and Christmas we glory in the beauty of that little baby in the manger, and well we should. However, we should not forget that this beautiful little baby was later disfigured beyond recognition, and that for our sin. As Isaiah says,

> ... there were many who were appalled at him—
> his appearance was so disfigured
>   beyond that of any man
> and his form marred beyond human likeness ...
> He had no beauty or majesty to attract us to him,
> nothing in his appearance that we should desire him.
> He was despised and rejected by men,
> a man of sorrows, and familiar with suffering.
> Like one from whom men hide their faces
> he was despised and we esteemed him not.
> Surely he took up our infirmities
>   and carried our sorrows ...
> But he was pierced for our transgressions,
>   he was crushed for our iniquities;
> the punishment that brought us peace was upon him.
>   (Isaiah 52:14; 53:2-5)

During this Advent and Christmas season, we need to spend time thinking about the price that Jesus came to pay for us. We need to be careful not to separate Christmas and the Cross.

TUESDAY OF THE FIRST WEEK

> "And I will put enmity
>   between you and the woman,
>   and between your offspring and hers;
> he will crush your head,
>   and you will strike his heel."

A third thing foretold by Genesis 3:15 is Christ's victory over Satan. Already in the Garden, God was revealing his plan to defeat Satan through Christ's life, death and resurrection, and offer salvation to the world through his Son. We must remember that a strike on the heel is not deadly, but a crushing blow to the head is.

As Matthew Henry once wrote, "Christ baffled Satan's temptations, rescued souls out of his hands. By his death He gave a fatal blow to the devil's kingdom, a wound to the head of this serpent that cannot be healed. As the gospel gains ground, Satan falls."

Christ's greatest victory is seen in the moment that seemed his greatest defeat: on the cross. In all this, the blessed Jesus, the seed of the woman, bruised Satan's accursed head. In that he was tempted, he is able to help those who are tempted. (Hebrews 4:18) By dying, he destroyed him that had the power of death, that is, the devil. (Hebrews 2:14) He thereby spoiled principalities and powers, and made a show of them openly, triumphing over them upon the cross. (Colossians 2:15) Furthermore, the Father sealed the Son's victory by raising him from the dead. The words—"he will crush your head" foreshadow Satan's defeat when Christ rose from the grave.

This reveals that no matter what difficulty we are going through right now, Christ can triumph over Satan even in the midst of our problems. The cross means that Jesus can turn every minus into a plus.

On Sunday, December 22, 1996, Carnell Taylor was working on a paving crew repairing the bridge on Interstate 64 over the Elizabeth River in Virginia. The road was icy, and a pickup truck slid out of control and hit Taylor, knocking him off the bridge. He fell seventy feet and hit the cold waters of the river below. His pelvis and some of the bones in his face were broken.

Joseph J. Brisson, the captain of a barge passing by at that moment, saw Taylor fall and quickly had to make a life-or-death decision. He knew Taylor would drown before he and his crew could launch their small boat and reach him. The numbingly cold water and strong currents of the river could kill him if he dove in to rescue Taylor. Brisson had a family, and Christmas was three days away.

Nonetheless, Brisson decided to risk his life for a man he had never met. He dove into the river, swam to Taylor, and grabbed hold of him. "Don't worry, buddy," he said, "I've got you." Brisson held Taylor's face above the water and encouraged him to keep talking. Then he took hold of a piece of wood in the water and slid it under Taylor to help keep him afloat. The current was too strong for them to swim to safety, and eventually the cold caused Brisson to lose his grip on Taylor. Therefore, Brisson wrapped his legs around the injured man's waist and held on.

After nearly thirty minutes the crew from the barge was finally able to reach the two men and pull them from the water into the boat. Taylor was hospitalized for broken bones. Brisson was treated for mild hypothermia.

In this perilous rescue, Joseph Brisson reveals something of the heart of God. Countless years ago, humans disobeyed God for the first time. As a result, human beings fell off a moral bridge into the icy waters of sin. However, God saw our plight. Thus, he dove into our world in order to rescue us. God became a human being, the seed of the woman, and was born that first Christmas day. In fact, God did more than subject himself to mild hypothermia. He subjected himself to death for our sake, to get us to safety; the serpent bruised his heal. However, the story didn't end there. Because of Christ's perfect life, and his precious sacrifice for our sin, the Father raised him from the freezing waters of death; through his death and resurrection, Christ crushed the head of the serpent. Think of it. If you had been the only one who ever fell into sin, the Son of God would have willingly left the safety and joy of his family in heaven to give himself for you.

C. S. Lewis put it this way, "In the Christian story God descends to re-ascend. He comes down; down from the heights of absolute being into time and space, down into humanity; down further still, if embryologists are right, to recapitulate in the womb ancient and pre-human phases of life; down to the very roots and sea-bed of the Nature He has created. But He goes down to come up again and bring the whole ruined world up with Him. One has the picture of the strong man stooping lower and lower to get himself underneath some great complicated burden. He must stoop in order to lift, he must almost disappear under the load before he incredibly straightens his back and marches off with the whole mass swaying on his shoulders. Or one may think of a diver, first reducing himself to nakedness, then glancing in mid-air, then gone with a splash, vanished, rushing down through green and warm water into black and cold water, down through increasing pressure into the death-like region of ooze and slime and old decay; then up again, back to colour and light, his lungs almost bursting, till suddenly he breaks surface again, holding in his hand the dripping, precious thing that he went down to recover. He and it are both coloured now that they have come up into the light: down below, where it lay colourless in the dark, he lost his colour too."[8]

You are that pearl of great price that the Son of God dove down to rescue. You are the reason that he became the seed of the woman. Your salvation was the reason why he allowed his heal to be bruised by the serpent. It was for you that he crushed the head of the serpent, so that you might be restored to paradise.

One day Christmas in paradise will no longer be an oxymoron. One day we will celebrate Christmas in paradise regained, because of Jesus' incarnation, death and resurrection. In the final judgment, the seed of the woman will give the last, fatal blow, crushing the serpent's head. Satan, the accuser of all Christians, will be cast into the lake of fire, and never suffered to disturb the seed of the woman any more. As Paul says in Romans 16:20, "The God of peace will soon crush Satan under your feet."

My dad died many years ago during Advent. As we drove down to be with my family for the funeral, my wife and I stopped at a restaurant. As I stood there in the tacky little restaurant gift shop looking at all the Christmas trinkets, I suddenly realized that my father would be celebrating Christmas in heaven, face to face with Jesus for the first time, because he had put his trust in Christ for salvation.

It is an awesome thought, but one day we too will be celebrating Christmas in paradise because of what Christ has done.

WEDNESDAY OF THE FIRST WEEK

Have you ever noticed how, when a man changes from being a candidate for President of the United States to actually being the President-elect or the President, suddenly his whole countenance changes? I have often thought it would be interesting to show before and after photos of each of the presidents. They always look much older, more tired, greyer, after serving in the Oval Office, don't they? I think that is because each president tries to bear the weight of the world on his shoulders.

I wonder: are you bearing the weight of the world on your shoulders? I know of a couple in the Bible who probably felt like they were bearing the weight of the world. That couple was Joseph and Mary. Try to imagine their situation.

Mary, at least, was most likely a teenager, yet she was engaged to Joseph, most likely an older man. Furthermore, engagement in that culture was a much more serious thing than in our culture. A Jewish betrothal period was almost like being married. The only way that such a betrothal could be broken was by divorce. In addition, sexual infidelity, or sex between the man and the woman who were betrothed, was looked at far more askance in Joseph and Mary's culture than it is in ours today.

So imagine what Mary must have felt when the angel told her that she was going to bear a child. Mary knew that she had never lain with a man. Thus, she asked the angel how this could be, and the angel told her that the Holy Spirit was going to conceive this child in her womb. However, then Mary must have asked herself, "What is Joseph going to think? Will he believe that this child is from God? Will he still love me and want to marry me? What will my family think? What will the neighbors think?" The weight of the world must have descended on Mary's shoulders when she received that announcement from the angel.

What about Joseph? When he first heard that Mary was pregnant, he planned to divorce her quietly. He could have made a big deal out of Mary's condition but he loved Mary and so he resolved to handle things discreetly.

Devotional Thoughts for the Holiday Season

What else could he do? He certainly couldn't go through with the marriage with Mary carrying someone else's child, could he?

Then an angel appears to Joseph and tells him not to be afraid to take Mary into his home as his wife because what is conceived in her is from the Holy Spirit. Now Joseph has a new burden to carry. He is glad to hear that Mary has been faithful to him, but then he learns that this child is to be named Jesus because he will save his people from their sins. How can he, a simple carpenter, be the stepfather, as it were, of the Savior of Israel? I'm sure that Joseph too felt the weight of the world on his shoulders after he received the angel's announcement.

George McCauslin was a man who was bearing the weight of the world on his shoulders. Dr. McCauslin was one of the greatest YMCA directors this world has ever seen. Some years ago, he was serving a YMCA in western Pennsylvania. In this YMCA that was losing membership, that had terrible financial difficulties and staff problems, George McCauslin found himself working 85 hours per week. He was getting little sleep at night. He took little time off and when he did have time off, he was thinking about the problems of this YMCA.

McCauslin went to a therapist who told him he was on the verge of a nervous breakdown. He had to learn somehow to let go and let God into his problems but he didn't know quite how to do that.

Therefore, one day, George McCauslin took the afternoon off. He took a pen and paper and went for a walk in the western Pennsylvania woods somewhere. As he walked through the cool forest, he could just feel his tight body and his stiff neck start to relax. He sat down under a tree and sighed. For the first time in months, he let go.

He took out his pen and paper, and decided he would release all the burdens in his life. He wrote God a letter and in that letter he said, "Dear God, today I hereby resign as general manager of the universe. Love, George."

George McCauslin, later describing this incident said, with a twinkle in his eye, "And wonder of wonders, God accepted my resignation."[9]

Are you trying to bear the weight of the world on your shoulders? Maybe you need to resign as general manager of the universe. Perhaps you are bearing the weight of health problems, or marriage breakdown or family difficulties or financial failure. Maybe your problem is with the holidays. Your life is so stressful right now, but you want everything to be just right for Christmas when the relatives are coming over. Nothing seems to be coming together and you are getting depressed about it.

Whatever your problem is, you need to know that Christ came to bear the weight of your world. You were never created to bear the weight of the world. He wants to bear that weight that you are trying, unsuccessfully, to

carry all by yourself.
    We read in Isaiah's prophecy of Christ . . .

> For to us a child is born,
> to us a son is given,
> *and the government will be on his shoulders.*
> And he will be called
> Wonderful Counselor, Mighty God,
> Everlasting Father, Prince of Peace.

THURSDAY OF THE FIRST WEEK

The child that was born to Mary was born for you. John Henry Jowett once wrote, "Who would have had sufficient daring of imagination to conceive that God Almighty would have appeared among men as a little child? We should have conceived something sensational, phenomenal, catastrophic, appalling! The most awful of the natural elements would have formed his retinue, and men would be chilled and frozen with fear. But, He came as a little child. The great God 'emptied Himself'; He let in the light as our eyes were able to bear it."

Jesus Christ was born for you and he was born to bear the government of the world on his shoulders. That includes the government of your life and your problems. He wants to bear it on his shoulders so that you won't be crushed by the weight.

Isaiah 9:6 mentions four names given to the Lord Jesus. As Billy Sunday once pointed out, "There are two hundred and fifty-six names given in the Bible for the Lord Jesus Christ, and I suppose this was because He was infinitely beyond all that any one name could express."

Do you need wisdom? Jesus Christ is a wonderful counselor. This title that is given to the Messiah, points to his role as king; he determines and carries out a program of action. As Wonderful Counselor, Christ is carrying out a royal program of bringing the world to himself. His program causes the world to marvel. If you need wisdom to deal with your problems, he is the best counselor that you can go to and he doesn't charge by the hour. All of his counsel is free.

However, as A.W. Tozer once said, "The present position of Christ in the gospel churches may be likened to that of a king in a limited constitutional monarchy. The king (sometimes depersonalized by the term 'the Crown') is in such a country no more than a traditional rallying point, a pleasant symbol of unity and loyalty much like a flag or a national anthem. He is lauded, feted, and supported, but his real authority is small. Nominally he is head over all, but in every crisis someone else makes the decisions. On formal occasions he appears in his royal attire to deliver the tame, colorless speech put into his mouth by the real rulers of the country. The whole thing may be no more than good-natured make-believe, but it is rooted in antiquity; it is a lot of fun, and no one wants to give it up."

Treating Christ like that is a waste of time and energy. Why not allow him to have the true reigns of authority to carry out his program in your life? His counsel will always be perfect.

Do you need someone to bear the weight of your problems? Christ is the one to do it because he is the **Mighty God**. This title stresses his divine power as warrior. Jesus will go to battle for you and in fact has gone to battle for you, winning the decisive victory against sin and Satan on the cross. Since he has all the power in the universe why don't you let him have a crack at your problems?

Sometimes when I am facing difficulties these days I wish my Dad were around to talk to. I wonder: Do you need a father to talk to who can give you encouragement and help you solve your problems? Jesus is the one to go to because he is the **Everlasting Father**. He is a father who won't run out on you. He is alive forevermore and he is constantly available to you if you have put your trust in him to save you from your sin. He is an enduring, compassionate provider and protector. He is the Everlasting Father.

Do you sometimes feel like your world is coming apart? Do you have wars within and wars without? Jesus can give you peace because he is the **Prince of Peace**. If you let him rule your life then he will bring you wholeness and wellbeing.

Michael Card has written, "All we could ever imagine, could ever hope for, He is… He is the Prince of Peace whose first coming has already transformed society but whose second coming will forever establish justice and righteousness. All this, and infinitely more, alive in an impoverished baby in a barn. That is what Christmas means—to find in a place where you would least expect to find anything you want, everything you could ever want."

However, as Addison Leitch once said, "Our trouble is we want the peace without the Prince." You can't have that. If you want peace in your life then you have to accept the Prince to get it. It's the only way.

The invitation is clear: allow Christ to bear the weight of your world. Make that decision today to roll off the weight on to his shoulders. Our problem as human beings is that we have to decide to do that every day, because we are constantly trying to take the weight of the world back on to our own shoulders. We resign as general managers of the universe for a day, but then we enlist ourselves again the next day in those same managerial roles.

There are two ways of handling problems in life when you come right down to it. One of those ways is pictured by the gigantic statue of Atlas that stands outside Rockefeller Center on Fifth Avenue in New York City. The statue shows a beautifully proportioned man, with all of his rippling muscles straining, holding the world upon his shoulders. That is one way to handle problems. You can try to carry it all on your shoulders. However, unlike Atlas, those problems will break you if you try to bear the weight yourself.

Another way to handle problems is illustrated just on the other side of Fifth Avenue in St. Patrick's Cathedral. Behind the high altar in the Cathedral there used to stand a little statue of the boy Jesus, perhaps eight or nine years old, and with no effort, he is holding a little globe, the world in fact, in one hand.[10]

Unto us a child is born. Unto us, a son is given, and the government shall be upon his shoulders.

Is the government of your life on your shoulders or his? You have a choice. You can try to carry the weight of the world and all your problems on your shoulders—and one day that weight will crush you, or you can allow Jesus Christ to carry the weight of your world.

FRIDAY OF THE FIRST WEEK

An article appeared in the Associated Press one December day a number of years ago: "Israel might declare Bethlehem a closed military area on Christmas Eve, preventing worshippers from arriving there....

"Bethlehem's mayor has already canceled Christmas Eve celebrations in the town because of more than two months of violence between Israelis and Palestinians. The violence has driven away most tourists, hitting Bethlehem's economy hard.

"The daily Maariv said Prime Minister Ehud Barak was considering imposing the restrictions if Palestinians do not stop firing on the Jewish neighborhood of Gilo, not far from Bethlehem. Israel television broadcast a similar report."

"O little town of Bethlehem, how still we see thee lie." Not so still these days, is it? But 2,700 years ago when Micah wrote his prophecy about the birth of the Messiah, Bethlehem was considerably more quiet, a seemingly insignificant place. Let us see what Micah has to say about the coming of the Messiah....

> But you, Bethlehem Ephrathah,
> though you are small among the clans of Judah,
> out of you will come for me
> one who will be ruler over Israel,
> whose origins are from of old,
> from ancient times. (Micah 5:2)

Who sent the Son of God into the world? An answer is suggested in the words of Micah 5:2. "Out of you," says the Lord speaking through the prophet Micah, "Out of you will come *for me*." God the Father sent his Son into the world.

God the Father sent his Son into the world that he might be the Savior of all. Too often, we ascribe the honor for our salvation to the Son of God alone. We picture God the Father as angry at us for our sin and God the Son as pacifying that anger. However, such is not the case. God the Father loves us, and chose to become incarnate in his Son. "For God so loved the world that he gave his one and only Son, that whoever believes in him shall not perish but have eternal life." (John 3:16)

Imagine the depth of love that the Father must have had for us that he gave himself for us in Jesus of Nazareth. I remember when my father laid his hand on my shoulder and prayed for me before I got in the car and left California to travel all the way across the country and go to seminary in Princeton, New Jersey. I remember another day, when once again I was moving from California, this time with a family of my own, to pastor a church in South Carolina. The day before I left, my father gave me a Scripture to guide me. I still have that Scripture, which he printed out for me on his computer, framed and hanging in my house to this day.

Partings between fathers and sons who love each other are not easy. I have a hard time letting my kids leave for school, or leave to go next door to play with their friends, or leave to go to a birthday party. It was even more difficult when I had to say goodbye to my eldest son and send him off to college.

The love that God the Father has for his Son is infinitely greater than the love that any of us as human fathers have for our human sons or daughters. Yet, he loved us so much that he was willing to give his Son for us. He didn't merely give his Son to travel across the country to go to college. No, he gave his Son to go from heaven to earth, from infinity to the finite, from spirit to occupying a body, from timeless eternity to the constraints of 24-hour days, from deity to humanity, from total life to death on a cross. When the Son of God left heaven, it had to be such an emotional parting that even the angels wept. They longed to be with the Son of God so much that they followed him down to earth just to watch and announce his birth.

I like the way Joseph Bayly put it in his Psalm for Christmas Eve . . .

> Praise God for Christmas.
> Praise Him for the Incarnation
> for Word made flesh.
> I will not sing
> of shepherds watching flocks
> on frosty night or angel choristers.
> I will not sing of stable bare in Bethlehem or lowing oxen
> wise men
> trailing distant star
> with gold and frankincense and myrrh.
> Tonight I will sing
> praise to the Father
> who stood on heaven's threshold

and said farewell to His Son
as He stepped across the stars
to Bethlehem
and Jerusalem.
And I will sing praise to the infinite eternal Son
who became most finite a Baby
who would one day be executed
for my crimes.
Praise Him in the heavens.
Praise Him in the stable.
Praise Him in my heart.

Who sent the Son of God into the world? God the Father sent him, and he did it out of love for us.

SATURDAY OF THE FIRST WEEK

Micah 5:2 answers another question. Where did the Son of God come to? He came to Bethlehem.

Today you can go to Bethlehem and see the place where Jesus was born. Thanks to Helena, the mother of the emperor Constantine, a church has been built over the site. Beneath the Church of the Nativity, a silver star marks the place where, it is believed, Christ was born. You have to walk down narrow steps into a dark grotto to get to the spot; all the way down, oil lamps hang from the ceiling of the cave. When I walked down there, I bumped my head on one of the lamps and got hot oil on my shirt. Talk about being anointed with oil—I was anointed. A stone slab, not far from the star, is supposed to mark the site of the manger where Jesus lay.

Malcolm Muggeridge once wrote, "Most of the shrines are doubtless fraudulent, some in dubious taste, and none to my liking. Yet one may note, as the visitors come and go, ranging from the devout to the inanely curious, that almost every face somehow lights up a little. Christ's presence makes itself felt even in this dubious birthplace."

We need to note that the Messiah was born in Bethlehem, first, *because of Bethlehem's history*. It is the town of David; the greatest King of Israel of all time was born there. All the Hebrew prophecies point to the fact that the Messiah would be from David's royal line. Therefore, the Christ had to be born in David's town.

The fact that the Messiah was born in Bethlehem is also interesting *because of Bethlehem's name*. Bethlehem means *House of Bread*. What more appropriate place could there be for the Bread of Life to be born than in the House of Bread? As Jesus later said, "I am the bread of life. He who comes to me will never go hungry, and he who believes in me will never be thirsty."

Do you hunger for something more in your life? Do you feel like your life is empty and that nothing can fill that emptiness—not even a happy family, a successful career, a nice house, and lots of money? Blaise Pascal once wrote:

> What else does this craving, and this helplessness, proclaim but that there was once in man a true happiness, of which all that now remains is the empty print and trace? This he tries in vain to fill with everything around him, seeking in things that are not there the help he cannot find in those that are though none can help, since this infinite abyss can be filled only with an infinite and immutable object; in other words by God himself. God alone is man's true good ...

Jesus is the only one who can ultimately satisfy our hunger for meaning, purpose, and for eternal life because he is the bread of life born in the house of bread.

A third thing to note about Bethlehem is the word that is added after it: Ephrathah. The word means fruitfulness or abundance. The name refers to the land around Bethlehem that made it a fruitful and abundant land agriculturally and that made Bethlehem a house of bread. How appropriate that Jesus was born in such a fruitful place because he is the only source of abundance in our lives. Jesus said, "I am the vine; you are the branches. If a man remains in me and I in him, he will bear much fruit; apart from me you can do nothing." We cannot produce anything in our lives that is lasting or truly beneficial without Jesus' help.

We must also recognize the significance of Jesus being born in Bethlehem as it relates to *Bethlehem's position*. "But you, Bethlehem Ephrathah, *though you are small* among the clans of Judah, out of you will come for me one who will be ruler over Israel . . ." Bethlehem was a small place in Micah's day. It was a small place in the time that Jesus was born and it is still a small place to this day. I remember standing on the outskirts of Bethlehem in 1984 and looking over the town and thinking, "What an amazing thing to happen in such an insignificant place—that the Son of God should be born in this out-of-the-way, one-horse town. They probably didn't even know what hit them."

The fact that the Son of God was born in a small place reminds us of the truth that Francis Schaeffer once pointed out in a sermon, and that is that there are *no little people and no little places* in God's scheme of things. Schaeffer wrote about how some people think:

> "It is wonderful to be a Christian, but I am such a small person, so limited in talents–or energy or psychological strength or knowledge– that what I do is not really important."

> The Bible, however, has quite a different emphasis: With God there are no little people.

Then Schaeffer goes on to say,

Devotional Thoughts for the Holiday Season

But if a Christian is consecrated, does this mean he will be in a big place instead of a little place? The answer, the next step, is very important: As there are no little people in God's sight, so there are no little places. To be wholly committed to God in the place where God wants him—this is the creature glorified.

Nowhere more than in America are Christians caught in the twentieth-century syndrome of size. Size will show success. If I am consecrated, there will necessarily be large quantities of people, dollars, etc. This is not so. Not only does God not say that size and spiritual power go together, but he even reverses this (especially in the teaching of Jesus) and tells us to be deliberately careful not to choose a place too big for us. We all tend to emphasize big works and big places, but all such emphasis is of the flesh. To think in such terms is simply to hearken back to the old, unconverted, egoist, self-centered *Me*. This attitude, taken from the world, is more dangerous to the Christian than fleshly amusement or practice. It is the flesh.

The Son of God came to earth, became a human being in a virgin's womb, and was born in a small place, partly to remind us that there are no little people and no little places. If we turn our life over to Christ's control, he can use us in a marvelous way, even if we think we are little people in a little place.

Many years ago in the city of Minneapolis at Bethlehem Baptist Church, they needed a Sunday school teacher for the junior boys. This class wasn't bad, just energetic. However, no teacher had been able to control them. Ewald Chaldberg, a Swedish masseur, was asked to teach, and he took the junior boys class.

Ewald still had his Swedish accent. Buzzing all over the church was the word, "He'll never make it. Three weeks, and that will be the end." However, somehow Ewald Chaldberg believed God when he took that class, and he stayed with it through the years. He kept teaching the boys everything he knew about the Lord.

Some years ago, that church celebrated the tenth anniversary of the death of Ewald Chaldberg. How do you like that—a layperson in the church, not even a pastor, and they were celebrating the tenth anniversary of his death.

During the service, they recounted that at least forty men were in Christian service some place in the world because Ewald Chaldberg taught boys, loved them, and watched over them as they grew. Ewald Chaldberg had faith to believe that God could overcome his human limitations.

On the morning of that anniversary celebration, twenty-seven laypeople stood up to say, "We're going to be like Ewald Chaldberg in a small way." That obscure immigrant with a Swedish accent found significance because he

Open Before Christmas

trusted the Lord who said, "My idea is bigger than your idea."

Because the Son of God came to earth and was born in the little town of Bethlehem, there are now no little people or little places if we follow him as our leader and forgiver.

THE SECOND SUNDAY OF ADVENT

What did the Son of God come to this world to do? Micah 5:2 tells us that the Messiah came to be "ruler over Israel." Jesus was *born* the king of the Jews as we learn from the story of the wise men in Matthew's Gospel.

Isn't that amazing? I can't think of one other person who was ever *born* a king. Some men are born princes, but never kings. They become kings. Prince William in England was born a prince, but he has yet to become a king. However, Jesus was the king of kings all along because he was and is the Son of God.

The real question is this: *is he ruler of our hearts?* Jesus is ruler over all things and people. Nothing can change that fact. However, we have a choice about whether we submit to his rule or not.

What happens when we do submit to his rule? I think the following story illustrates at least a partial answer to that question....

There was a man who grew up in a Christian home. The man's father was a preacher, so the man learned how to talk the talk of the Christian life, but walking the walk was another matter.

At the age of nineteen, the man committed armed robbery and was sent to jail. After his release, he served in the army during World War II. After rising to the rank of captain, the man suddenly found himself facing a court martial for misuse of priorities and misappropriation of government property. He was sentenced to ten years in a federal penitentiary.

After serving two years, the man received a presidential pardon from Harry Truman, and was ordered to continue serving in the Army Air Force, lecturing around the United States on his topic of expertise—electronics—specifically radar and communications.

Upon receiving an honorable discharge, the man returned to his home in Los Angeles where he married and started an electronic engineering business. Because of his unique talent for wiretapping, this man was soon working for the Los Angeles Police Department, helping to bust prostitution in the city. In addition, he worked for a private detective, performing wiretapping and electronic eavesdropping for many famous movie stars, prominent businesspeople and politicians.

This work attracted the attention of Mickey Cohen who, at that time, was the "godfather" of organized crime in Southern California. Cohen summoned the wire-tapper to his office on Sunset Boulevard and began firing questions.

"Did you place a listening device in my home?"

"No, Mr. Cohen I didn't. I don't even know where you live," the man replied.

"Well, if there was a listening device in my home, could you come and remove it?" Cohen queried.

The man thought for a moment. "You don't understand, Mr. Cohen. I'm in the business of installing listening devices. I don't ever take them out."

Cohen reached into his pocket and pulled out a roll of hundred dollar bills. He began peeling them off, one at a time. "Does this change your mind?"

"I think my business is about to expand," the man answered nonchalantly.

That job led to others. Soon the wire-tapper was working both for Cohen and the LAPD simultaneously. However, eventually, the man gave up his work with the police and worked for Cohen full time. After all, Cohen paid better, and in cash. Thus, there was no need to report his income to the Internal Revenue Service.

Through Cohen, the wire-tapper met others in organized crime very keen to utilize his talents. St. Louis Andy asked the wire-tapper to develop a system for past-post betting on the racehorses. The wire-tapper complied by putting together an electronic system to withhold race results coming over the Continental Wire Service. The wire-tapper set up the system in Arizona to intercept and withhold for ninety seconds race results entering Southern California over the wire. This was just enough time for St. Louis Andy to notify his operatives in Southern California of the horses that had won races in other parts of the country. These henchmen placed bets on the winning horses in illegal off-track betting houses and came up winners every time. (If the story sounds familiar, that may be because it became the subject of the Oscar award-winning film, *The Sting*, starring Paul Newman and Robert Redford.)

The wire-tapper was scheduled to travel to St. Louis on November 10, 1949, to set up his electronic system to control all the illegal off-track betting in the western part of the United States. However, he didn't make that visit to St. Louis because on November 6, the wire-tapper and his wife happened to attend a tent meeting on the corner of Washington and Hill in Los Angeles where a young preacher named Billy Graham was speaking.

That night, Mr. Graham quoted the question of Jesus: "What shall it profit a man if he gain the whole world but lose his own soul?" Then, at the end of his message, Mr. Graham said, "There is a man in this audience tonight who has heard this message many times before, but he has never given his life to Christ, and this may be his last opportunity."

The wire-tapper sensed that God was speaking directly to him. He got up from his seat and walked the sawdust trail to the prayer tent where he knelt and prayed, "God, if you'll mean business with me, then I'll mean business with you. If you can take my twisted life and straighten it out, then I'll give it all to you."

The man who knelt in that prayer tent and committed his life to follow Jesus Christ was my father, Jim Vaus. From that day forward, my father set about making everything right with people he had wronged. He quit organized crime altogether and repaid everyone he had ever cheated. When restitution was complete, my parents had nothing left, no home and no car, but God began to provide for them, sometimes in miraculous ways.

My father spent the rest of his life sharing with others the positive power of Jesus Christ that had changed his own life. In 1958, he started a Christian outreach to teenage gangs in New York City, a ministry that eventually spanned the country.

My father's life is just one example of the change that can happen to any person when they surrender to the rule of Jesus Christ. For the first thirty years of his life, my father talked the talk of Christianity. However, in 1949 when he surrendered his life to Christ's control, he began to walk the walk.

How about you? Are you just talking the talk of Christianity, or are you indeed walking the walk?

MONDAY OF THE SECOND WEEK

Micah 5:2 also raises the question about the Son of God: did he ever come before? The answer is an amazing: yes! The Son of God had his origins from eternity: "Whose origins are from of old, from ancient times."

That phrase, "from of old," can also be translated "from days of eternity." God did not become a tri-personal being when Christ was born in Bethlehem. God has always existed as three persons in one being. The Son of God has always existed and always been proceeding from God the Father. He is *eternally* begotten of the Father, as the Nicene Creed puts it, and the Holy Spirit has always been proceeding from the Father and the Son.

I believe the Son of God even appeared to people in Old Testament times, assuming a human form. The Son of God met Abraham when the Lord was about to destroy Sodom and Gomorrah for their wickedness. Abraham pleaded with the Lord to save his nephew Lot and his family who lived in Sodom.

The Son of God appeared to Abraham's grandson Jacob at a critical point in his life when he was about to meet his brother Esau again after long years of separation. Jacob knew that his brother Esau had been mad enough to kill him when he left home years before. God met Jacob in human form and wrestled with him through the night.

The Son of God appeared to Joshua, the leader of Israel's armies, right before they were going to battle against Jericho to recapture Palestine for God's people. The Son of God appeared to Joshua as a soldier and made Joshua realize that God was the one in command of the army at this critical juncture in Joshua's life.

The Lord appeared in human form to the young Hebrews—Shadrach, Meshach and Abednego—when they were thrown into the fiery furnace because they would not bow down before the statue of King Nebuchadnezzar. The Son of God walked with those three young Hebrews in the fiery furnace. Because God was with them, they were not burned.

It is interesting to note that in every instance where the Son of God appeared in human form to people in the Hebrew Scriptures, it was always at a very critical juncture in their lives. He did not meet them at points of ease or prosperity. He met them at points where they were praying about life and death matters, or when they were about to go into battle, or when they were suffering persecution. The same holds true today. You say, "I would like to meet God face to face. Then I will believe." You may not like what will have to happen to you before you can meet God face to face. The Lord has to bring us to the end of ourselves before we can meet him and truly begin to know him in a personal way.

Yes, I believe the Son of God came to earth many times before his incarnation in Bethlehem. He could do that because he has always existed. Furthermore, he can come again now into our lives if we will admit him. As Corrie ten Boom once said, "If Jesus were born one thousand times in Bethlehem and not in me, then I would still be lost."

Therefore, we need to allow Christ to be born in our hearts today. We need to invite him to be our ruler and our forgiver. We must ask him to become the bread of life to us, so that our lives can be a house of bread in which he can dwell.

Corrie ten Boom is a great example of someone who received Jesus as the bread of life and whose life consequently became a house of bread for others. During World War II, Corrie and her family housed Jews in their home in Holland, hiding them from the Nazis. As a result, the ten Booms were carted off to a prison camp where Corrie's father and sister died.

However, before her death, Corrie's sister Betsie taught her a very important lesson. Corrie wrote about it in her book, *The Hiding Place*, where she tells about lying down in her bunk in Barracks 28 at Ravensbruck for the first time….

> "Fleas!" I cried. "Betsie, the place is swarming with them!" …
>
> "Show us. Show us how." It was said so matter of factly it took me a second to realize she was praying. More and more the distinction between prayer and the rest of life seemed to be vanishing for Betsie.
>
> "Corrie!" she said excitedly. "He's given us the answer! Before we asked, as He always does! In the Bible this morning. Where was it? Read that part again!"
>
> I glanced down the long dim aisle to make sure no guard was in sight, then drew the Bible from its pouch. "It was in First Thessalonians," I said. We were on our third complete reading of the New Testament since leaving Scheveningen.
>
> In the feeble light I turned the pages. "Here it is: 'Comfort the frightened, help the weak, be patient with everyone. See that none of you repays evil for evil, but always seek to do good to one another and

to all...'" It seemed written expressly for Ravensbruck.

"Go on," said Betsie. "That wasn't all."

"Oh yes: 'Rejoice always, pray constantly, give thanks in all circumstances; for this is the will of God in Christ Jesus.'"

"That's it, Corrie! That's His answer. 'Give thanks in all circumstances!' That's what we can do. We can start right now to thank God for every single thing about this new barracks!" I stared at her; then around me at the dark, foul-aired room.

"Such as?" I said.

"Such as being assigned here together."

I bit my lip. "Oh yes, Lord Jesus!"

"Such as what you're holding in your hands." I looked down at the Bible.

"Yes! Thank You, dear Lord, that there was no inspection when we entered here! Thank You for all these women, here in this room, who will meet You in these pages."

"Yes," said Betsie, "Thank You for the very crowding here. Since we're packed so close, that many more will hear!" She looked at me expectantly. "Corrie!" she prodded.

"Oh, all right. Thank You for the jammed, crammed, stuffed, packed suffocating crowds."

"Thank You," Betsie went on serenely, "for the fleas and for—"

The fleas! This was too much. "Betsie, there's no way even God can make me grateful for a flea."

"Give thanks in all circumstances," she quoted. "It doesn't say, 'in pleasant circumstances.' Fleas are part of this place where God has put us."

And so we stood between tiers of bunks and gave thanks for fleas. But this time I was sure Betsie was wrong....

They were services like no others, these times in Barracks 28.

At first Betsie and I called these meetings with great timidity. But as night after night went by and no guard ever came near us, we grew bolder. So many now wanted to join us that we held a second service after evening roll call. There on the Lagerstrasse we were under rigid surveillance, guards in their warm wool capes marching constantly up and down. It was the same in the center room of the barracks: half a dozen guards or camp police always present. Yet in the large dormitory room there was almost no supervision at all. We did not understand it.

One evening I got back to the barracks late from a wood-gathering foray outside the walls. A light snow lay on the ground and it was hard to find the sticks and twigs with which a small stove was kept going in each room. Betsie was waiting for me, as always, so that we could wait through the food line together. Her eyes were twinkling.

"You're looking extraordinarily pleased with yourself,' I told her.

"You know, we've never understood why we had so much freedom in the big room," she said. "Well—I've found out."

That afternoon, she said, there'd been confusion in her knitting group about sock sizes and they'd asked the supervisor to come and settle it.

But she wouldn't. She wouldn't step through the door and neither would the guards. "And you know why?"

Betsie could not keep the triumph from her voice: "Because of the fleas! That's what she said, 'That place is crawling with fleas!'"

My mind rushed back to our first hour in this place. I remembered Betsie's bowed head, remembered her thanks to God for creatures I could see no use for.

Sometimes the Son of God meets us in the strangest and darkest of places and protects us in unusual ways. In the places where we are most hungry, he is the bread of life for us—bread he calls us to offer to others as well.

TUESDAY OF THE SECOND WEEK

Who can endure Christmas? By that I mean, who can endure the commercial racket of it all? By Christmas Eve I am sure we are all tired of all the gift buying, the laying on of extra food for the holiday, the attendance at holiday school plays and concerts, the sending of Christmas cards (if we have even gotten around to that), and the endless round of parties. Aren't we all ready for some peace and quiet and time to just think about the real meaning of Christmas?

C. S. Lewis wrote to a friend at Christmastime: "I seem to have been writing Christmas letters most of this day! I'm afraid I hate the weeks just before Christmas, and so much of the (very commercialised and vulgarised) fuss has nothing to do with the Nativity at all… To tell a story which puts the contrast between *our* feast of the Nativity and, all this ghastly 'Xmas' racket at its lowest. My brother heard a woman on a bus say, as the bus passed a church with a Crib outside it, 'Oh, Lor'! They bring religion into everything. Look—they're dragging it even into Christmas now!'"

Who can endure Christmas? The prophet Malachi asks an even more pointed question in the book that bears his name. He asks, "But who can endure the day of his coming? Who can stand when he appears?" The "he" to whom Malachi refers is none other than the Messiah whose birth we celebrate at Christmas and the one whose Second Coming every true Christian should eagerly prepare for.

Let us read again together Malachi's prophecy and see what we can learn about how to prepare for Christ's coming, the purpose of his coming, and the result of his coming.

> "See, I will send my messenger, who will prepare the way before me. Then suddenly the Lord you are seeking will come to his temple; the messenger of the covenant, whom you desire, will come," says the Lord Almighty.
>
> But who can endure the day of his coming? Who can stand when he

appears? For he will be like a refiner's fire or a launderer's soap. He will sit as a refiner and purifier of silver; he will purify the Levites and refine them like gold and silver. Then the LORD will have men who will bring offerings in righteousness, and the offerings of Judah and Jerusalem will be acceptable to the LORD, as in days gone by, as in former years.

The first thing that Malachi talks about here is the preparation for the coming of the Messiah. It was the practice in the Near East to send messengers in advance of a visiting king to announce his coming and to remove all hindrances or obstacles. The Lord sent a messenger to prepare the way for the Messiah; that messenger was John the Baptist.

Malachi's words have reference both to Christ's first coming two thousand years ago and to his Second Coming which is still future. Charles Spurgeon once wrote,

> Jesus' first coming was without external pomp or show of power, yet there were few who endured its testing. Herod and all Jerusalem were stirred at the news of the wondrous birth, but many who were waiting for Him showed their hypocrisy by rejecting Him when He came.
>
> His life on earth was a separating fan, and when it tried the great heap of religious profession, few endured the process. But what will His second advent be like? What sinner can endure to think of it? 'He shall strike the earth with the rod of His mouth, and with the breath of His lips He shall slay the wicked.' (Isaiah 11:4)
>
> When in His humiliation He only had to say, 'I am He,' and the soldiers fell to the ground (John 18:6), what, then, will it be like for His enemies when He shall be fully revealed as 'I AM' (Exodus 3:14)?
>
> His death shook the earth and darkened heaven (Luke 23:44). What, then, will be the dreadful splendor of that day when, as the living Savior, He shall summon the living and the dead before Him (2 Timothy 4:1)?

How can we prepare for Christ's Second Coming? We can prepare in the same way people prepared for his first coming—by following John the Baptist's instructions. In Matthew 3:1-10 we read,

> In those days John the Baptist came, preaching in the Desert of Judea and saying, "Repent, for the kingdom of heaven is near." This is he who was spoken of through the prophet Isaiah:
>
> > "A voice of one calling in the desert,
> > 'Prepare the way for the Lord,
> > make straight paths for him.'"
>
> John's clothes were made of camel's hair, and he had a leather belt

around his waist. His food was locusts and wild honey. People went out to him from Jerusalem and all Judea and the whole region of the Jordan. Confessing their sins, they were baptized by him in the Jordan River.

But when he saw many of the Pharisees and Sadducees coming to where he was baptizing, he said to them: "You brood of vipers! Who warned you to flee from the coming wrath? Produce fruit in keeping with repentance. And do not think you can say to yourselves, 'We have Abraham as our father.' I tell you that out of these stones God can raise up children for Abraham. The ax is already at the root of the trees, and every tree that does not produce good fruit will be cut down and thrown into the fire.

We need to prepare for Christ's coming by repentance, which means turning from sin. We need to prepare by confessing our sin. We need to prepare by living a life in keeping with repentance, lives that demonstrate righteousness. The purple color that we see on our advent candles is there to remind us of our need for repentance from sin. Purple is the color of penance. Just as John the Baptist was the messenger who came before the King to remove any obstacles to his arrival, so we too need to remove the obstacles to Christ living in our lives.

In an interview with Will Norton, Jr., best-selling novelist John Grisham recalls:

> One of my best friends in college died when he was 25, just a few years after we had finished Mississippi State University. I was in law school, and he called me one day and wanted to get together. So we had lunch, and he told me he had terminal cancer.
>
> I couldn't believe it. I asked him, 'What do you do when you realize that you are about to die?'
>
> He said, 'It's real simple. You get things right with God, and you spend as much time with those you love as you can. Then you settle up with everybody else.' Then he said, 'You know, really, you ought to live every day like you have only a few more days to live.'

What a true statement! We need to be ready at all times, not only for our own death, but also for Christ's Second Coming. For when he comes, as Malachi tells us, it will be sudden.

WEDNESDAY OF THE SECOND WEEK

The purpose of Christ's Coming, both his first and second comings, according to Malachi, is to refine and purify.

Think about what Jesus did at his first coming. He did not remain a cute little baby in the manger. He grew up to be a man, who would later come to the Temple and throw out the moneychangers. Not only that, but Jesus purified the sacrifices of the temple by his perfect sacrifice on the cross for our sins.

When Jesus comes again to judge the earth, he will purge his people once for all of sin. That purging process is something that begins in the life of every Christian the moment we trust in Christ to save us from our sin.

We must note that this refining and purifying process hurts. Nobody likes being burned by fire. A launderer's soap can burn if it is like the alkali that Malachi refers to. Jesus' purpose for being born at Christmas was something like what Tom Landry once described as the job of a football coach. "The job of a football coach is to make men do what they don't want to do, in order to achieve what they've always wanted to be."

God created us in his image. However, sin has marred that image. Now it takes pain to restore that full image in us. Sometimes that purifying pain comes in the form of repeated failure and heartache in life.

When he was seven years old, his family was forced out of their home on a legal technicality, and he had to work to help support them. At age nine, his mother died. At 22, he lost his job as a store clerk. He wanted to go to law school, but his previous education wasn't good enough. At 23, he went into debt to become a partner in a small store. At 26, his business partner died, leaving him a huge debt that took years to repay. At 28, after courting a girl for four years, he asked her to marry him. She said no. At 37, on his third try, he was elected to Congress, but two years later, he failed to be re-elected. At 41, his four-year-old son died. At 45, he ran for the Senate and lost. At 47, he failed as the vice-presidential candidate. At 49, he ran for the Senate again, and lost. At 51, he was elected President of the United States. His name was Abraham Lincoln, perhaps the greatest president our nation has ever had.

Some people get all the breaks, huh? No, Abraham Lincoln's life was purified by pain.

Malachi makes it clear that the refining and purifying process starts with leaders. Malachi says that the Messiah will purify the Levites and refine them like gold and silver. The Levites were the ones charged with taking care of things in the temple and presenting sacrifices to the Lord. These Levites hadn't done their job right. They had led people astray. Thus, Malachi says that the purifying process that the Messiah would carry out would begin with them. That is the way it always works. To purify an organization you must begin with the leaders.

Don Stevenson, President of Global Hospitality, says there are two things he always does when he takes over a resort that has been failing. He fires the president and he trains the people who are out front meeting customers.

In a church that has been failing, it works the same way. The leadership has to change. It has to be purified.

Perhaps the purification in Abraham Lincoln's life as a leader enabled him to lead our country through the purifying pain of the War Between the States.

In any case, what we need to see is that *the final product of purifying pain is worth it*. That final product is to become like the Lord. Here is what a silversmith had to say about refining silver:

"I must sit with my eyes steadily fixed on the furnace; for if the time necessary for refining be exceeded in the slightest degree, the silver will be injured. I never take my eye off the silver in the furnace. If I take it out too early, it won't be purified. If I leave it in too late, it will be injured. When the silver is in the fire, I focus. I don't let anything distract me. I watch that silver, carefully waiting for the right moment to take it out."

When is the right moment? The silversmith says, "I know the silver is pure when I can see my face reflected there."

John Maxwell has written, "When I'm in a storm, as soon as the storm comes, I'm saying, 'Okay, God, bail me out. Find me. Rescue me!' Sometimes He doesn't rescue me. He doesn't come. But He is the great silversmith. While I'm in the furnace, He focuses and watches. His job isn't a quick rescue mission. His job is to purify. He holds me until the right moment, and then He comes—never too early, never too late—right on time."

Are you going through a refining, purifying experience of pain right now? That is what Jesus was born to do. He came to purify your life by his perfect life, his death on the cross for your sin, and his resurrection from the dead. Trust Him. He will not leave you in the furnace of affliction any longer than is necessary. He has his eye on you. He loves you. He wants to purify your life completely, and he will do it.

Would you dare to make your prayer the same as that of George Whitefield? "O may God put me into one furnace after another, that my soul may be transparent; that I may see God as he is."

THURSDAY OF THE SECOND WEEK

Malachi also tells us about the result of Christ's coming: the giving of righteous gifts to the Lord. "Then the Lord will have men who will bring offerings in righteousness, and the offerings of Judah and Jerusalem will be acceptable to the Lord, as in days gone by, as in former years." Jesus was born that first Christmas to purify our lives from sin so that we in turn may offer our lives back to him as living sacrifices. The offering that he wants is prayer, thanksgiving, and self-dedication.

Paul says, "Therefore, I urge you, brothers, in view of God's mercy, to offer your bodies as living sacrifices, holy and pleasing to God–this is your spiritual act of worship." (Romans 12:1) The writer to the Hebrews says, "Through Jesus, therefore, let us continually offer to God a sacrifice of praise—the fruit of lips that confess his name." (Hebrews 13:15)

One Sunday morning a six-year-old boy was busy getting dressed for Sunday school. When it was time for his family to leave for church, he came out of his room carrying his entire stock of neckties. When his mother asked him why he was doing this, he eagerly replied, "Cause, Mom, Pastor told us to put our ties in the offering!" The Bible does talk about our giving "tithes", a tenth of our income, but I think the Lord is more interested in our giving of ourselves to him.

What gift can you give back to the one who was born at Christmas to purify you from your sin? I think the following story helps to answer that question.

In 1994, two Americans answered an invitation from the Russian Department of Education to teach morals and ethics (based upon biblical principles) in the public schools. They were invited to teach at prisons, businesses, the fire and police departments and a large orphanage. About one hundred boys and girls who had been abandoned, abused, and left in the care of a government-run program were in the orphanage. Those two Americans relate the following story....

Devotional Thoughts for the Holiday Season

It was nearing the holiday season, 1994, time for our orphans to hear, for the first time, the traditional story of Christmas. We told them about Mary and Joseph arriving in Bethlehem. Finding no room in the inn, the couple went to a stable, where the baby Jesus was born and placed in a manger. Throughout the story, the children and orphanage staff sat in amazement as they listened. Some sat on the edges of their stools, trying to grasp every word.

Completing the story, we gave the children three small pieces of cardboard to make a crude manger. Each child was given a small paper square, cut from yellow napkins I had brought with me. No colored paper was available in the city. Following instructions, the children tore the paper and carefully laid strips in the manger for straw. Small squares of flannel, cut from a worn-out nightgown an American lady was throwing away as she left Russia, were used for the baby's blanket. A doll-like baby was cut from tan felt we had brought from the United States.

The orphans were busy assembling their manger as I walked among them to see if they needed any help. All went well until I got to one table where little Misha sat. He looked to be about 6 years old and had finished his project. As I looked at the little boy's manger, I was startled to see not one, but two babies in the manger.

Quickly, I called for the translator to ask the lad why there were two babies in the manger. Crossing his arms in front of him and looking at his completed manger scene, the child began to repeat the story very seriously. For such a young boy, who had only heard the Christmas story once, he related the happenings accurately—until he came to the part where Mary put the baby Jesus in the manger. Then Misha started to ad-lib.

He made up his own ending to the story as he said, 'And when Maria laid the baby in the manger, Jesus looked at me and asked me if I had a place to stay. I told him I have no mamma and I have no papa, so I don't have any place to stay. Then Jesus told me I could stay with him. But I told him I couldn't, because I didn't have a gift to give him like everybody else did. But I wanted to stay with Jesus so much, so I thought about what I had that maybe I could use for a gift. I thought maybe if I kept him warm, that would be a good gift.

'So I asked Jesus, 'If I keep you warm, will that be a good enough gift?'

'And Jesus told me, 'If you keep me warm, that will be the best gift anybody ever gave me.'

Open Before Christmas

'So I got into the manger, and then Jesus looked at me and he told me I could stay with him–for always.'

As little Misha finished his story, his eyes brimmed full of tears that splashed down his little cheeks. Putting his hand over his face, his head dropped to the table and his shoulders shook as he sobbed and sobbed. The little orphan had found someone who would never abandon nor abuse him, someone who would stay with him—FOR ALWAYS.

What can you give this Christmas to the one who came to purify you from your sin? I think Christina Rosetti put it best in her poem....

> "What can I give Him,
> Poor as I am?
> If I were a shepherd,
> I would bring a lamb,
> If I were a Wise Man,
> I would do my part—
> Yet what can I give Him?
> Give my heart."

Give the Lord your heart this Christmas. Let him purify your life of sin. Allow him to prepare you for his second coming that will be even better than his first.

FRIDAY OF THE SECOND WEEK

What does Christmas mean for you? In a December issue of a leading magazine the following ads were displayed:

- "What greater treasure of Christmas could you give than sheets and pillowcases?"
- "Crowning gift of all: Our lovebird scarf of Russian sable, $9,000."
- "Christmas everywhere! And in America it's—Cashmeres."

Does Christmas simply mean a time for giving gifts to one another?

Perhaps for you there is a deeper meaning to Christmas. Maybe for you, Christmas is supremely a time for family: a time to "go home for the holidays". Christmas to you may mean the warmth and love of home.

On the other hand: Christmas for you may mean one long line of parties. You run here. You dash there. Perhaps Christmas is one unending, disjointed bit of superficial conversation shared over eggnog.

Yet again: Christmas for you may be a time to do something for others who can't do much for themselves. That is a wonderful focus to have at Christmas as well as all year round.

However, I would like to suggest to you that Christmas is much more than any of these things. Christmas is, foremost, a birthday. It is the birthday of King Jesus. That is what we read about in Matthew 1:18-25….

> This is how the birth of Jesus Christ came about: His mother Mary was pledged to be married to Joseph, but before they came together, she was found to be with child through the Holy Spirit. Because Joseph her husband was a righteous man and did not want to expose her to public disgrace, he had in mind to divorce her quietly.
>
> But after he had considered this, an angel of the Lord appeared to him in a dream and said, "Joseph son of David, do not be afraid to take Mary home as your wife, because what is conceived in her is from the

Holy Spirit. She will give birth to a son, and you are to give him the name Jesus, because he will save his people from their sins."

All this took place to fulfill what the Lord had said through the prophet: "The virgin will be with child and will give birth to a son, and they will call him Immanuel"—which means, "God with us."

When Joseph woke up, he did what the angel of the Lord had commanded him and took Mary home as his wife. But he had no union with her until she gave birth to a son. And he gave him the name Jesus.

The birth of King Jesus brought change to world history. His birth brought a change in our calendars. Now all events in history are dated according to BC or AD. Some scholars have changed that method of dating to BCE and CE, "before the common era" and "common era". Still, history has been changed by the birth of Christ.

What are the personal implications of Christ's birth? What changes will result in our lives if Christ is born and growing in us?

First, I believe the birth of King Jesus in our lives will mean *a change in plans*. Mary and Joseph had to change their plans dramatically because of the birth of Jesus into their lives.

Mary was "pledged to be married" to Joseph. This meant that Mary and Joseph would be referred to as husband and wife, but they would not have come together to have any sexual relationship. They would not yet have been living together in the same house. In fact, Joseph may have been working at this time on building the house in which he and Mary would live.

Think of how Joseph and Mary's plans must have been disrupted by the birth of Jesus into their lives at that time. I am sure they must have been looking forward to time alone together. Then suddenly Joseph finds out that Mary is pregnant. The Scripture does not tell us how Joseph found out. Presumably, Mary told him. Can you imagine how difficult that conversation must have been? The Scripture tells us nothing of Mary trying to tell Joseph about the miraculous conception of this child. Perhaps Joseph was not ready to hear about it. All he could see was that Mary was having a baby that was not his, and that this spelled the end of their relationship. All of his plans were changed. His hopes were dashed.

If Jesus is born and growing in our lives, then there will be disruption for us as well. Once Jesus comes in, we cannot go on with life as it has always been. All of us naturally want to control our own lives. We may have all our plans made for what we want to do. However, then, Jesus comes and asks to take control, and he deserves to do so, doesn't he? After all, he is the King. Yet, even as Christians, we try to make Jesus conform to our plans rather than making our lives conform to his plan. James Dittes once wrote,

Devotional Thoughts for the Holiday Season

For it is not easy for Christ to come to us, nor for us to serve him, when our lives are neat and stable. We try so hard to be strong men and undivided and to bind the Lord, his church, his ministry, in swaddling cloths, and to lay them in a stable place. But our full and ordered house shuts them out—just as the inn at Bethlehem. Perhaps it is just to a divided nation, a ruptured community, a torn family, a split self, a chaotic sense of vocation, an impossible church, that Christ and his call comes.

If Jesus has been born into our lives then there is going to be disruption, there is going to be a change of plans.

SATURDAY OF THE SECOND WEEK

If Jesus has been born in our lives, there will also be *a change in righteousness*. I think Jesus' conception caused Joseph to rethink his concept of holiness. Matthew tells us that Joseph was a righteous man and did not want to expose Mary to public disgrace. Therefore, he decided to divorce her quietly.

If Mary had conceived a child by another man during betrothal then it would have been adultery. Betrothal was a serious engagement. The only way it could be broken was by divorce. Years before this, Mary's apparent act would have been punishable by stoning, but the Jewish legislation in this regard had been tempered by this time. Thus, Joseph had two conventional choices. Either he could expose Mary to the humiliation of a public trial, or he could divorce her quietly—signing the necessary legal papers.

The Scripture says that Joseph was a righteous man. In other words, he sought to obey God's law as best he could. According to Joseph's concept of righteousness, he would have to divorce Mary, even though he loved her. There was no other way to resolve the matter according to conventional wisdom. However, Joseph's understanding of the law as well as his own heart, dictated to him that he should be merciful.

All that changed after Joseph's encounter with the angel. He was challenged to live out a kind of holiness deeper than this superficial, legalistic righteousness. Joseph was prompted by the messenger from God to do something radical. He was asked to take Mary as his wife. Joseph's family and friends would, most likely, not understand his choice, given the situation. Why would any man, in that day and age, take as his wife a woman who was with child by another man? It was unthinkable. However, once Joseph received the revelation from the angel about the identity of the child in Mary's womb, Joseph opted for radical righteousness. He simply did what the Lord told him to do, even though he knew no one, other than Mary, would understand or agree with his decision.

I believe God wants us to live out a deeper righteousness. Being Christians does not mean that we are members of the Kingdom of Niceness. Our king calls us to do some radical things. However, in real life, most of us prefer to play it safe.

Wilbur Rees has written:

> I would like to buy $3 worth of God, please, not enough to explode my soul or disturb my sleep, but just enough to equal a cup of warm milk or a snooze in the sunshine. I don't want enough of Him to make me love a black man or pick beets with a migrant. I want ecstasy, not transformation; I want the warmth of the womb, not a new birth. I want a pound of the Eternal in a paper sack. I would like to buy $3 worth of God, please.

What demonstration of radical righteousness is God calling each one of us to perform? Maybe it is saying "no" to certain unethical practices in the workplace. Perhaps it is reaching out to neighbors or co-workers who know nothing of Christ, rather than remaining comfortable in our holy huddle at church. I don't know what act of radical righteousness God is calling you to perform. However, I imagine each of us can think of some areas in our lives where we need to go deeper in our commitment to the king and his kingdom. I pray that the Lord will give you courage to respond to his calling, whatever that calling may be.

THE THIRD SUNDAY OF ADVENT

A third change, which will be taking place in our lives if Jesus has been born in our hearts, is *a change of focus*. The angel told Joseph that the Holy Spirit conceived the child in Mary's womb. He also told Joseph that this child should be named "Jesus" because he would save his people from their sins.

The name "Jesus" means "Yahweh saves". "Yahweh" is the personal name of God. It can be translated simply as: "I am". God is the self-existent One; he is not dependent upon anyone or anything else but himself. Thus, the name "Jesus" means: "I am" saves.

Many Jewish children at the time of our Lord's birth were named "Jesus". "Jesus" is the Greek transliteration of the Hebrew name "Yeshua" or "Joshua". Thus, the name of Mary's child was not unique. However, when combined with the other things that the angel told Joseph about this child, it is clear that this child *was* to be unique. He was given the name "Jesus" by an angel for a unique reason. The angel said the reason for the name was that he would save his people from their sins.

What is sin? This may seem like a very basic question, but sometimes we need to go back to basics. The word in the Greek means simply to fall short of the mark. God has set a certain mark, a certain standard for our lives, and we all fall short of it. Romans 3:23 says, "All have sinned and fallen short of the glory of God."

Sin is, basically, self-centeredness. God created us to be centered in him, to have him as our focal point. However, we have all become self-centered, both by heredity and by choice. The good news is that Jesus has come, and by his birth, life, death, resurrection and intercession at the right hand of the Father, he enables us to return to a God-centered focus in life.

The story is told of an alcoholic who became so intoxicated one night that he stumbled through the open door of a stable. He woke up the next morning bewildered by his strange surroundings. Finally, it dawned on him where he was. He was very hungry and so tried to think of a neighbor who might give him a meal. "No," he muttered, "I'm afraid they'd say I've fallen too low." Just then, he heard some bells ringing, and he suddenly realized it was Christmas

Day. "What was that story again? About shepherds, the manger, a child born in a stable and an angel's message? I'm not the first one to sleep in a stable," he thought. Recalling his childhood training in Christianity, he remembered that God had come into the world through Jesus to save his people from their sin. He wondered and pondered, "Had Jesus appeared in a stable to remind the world that the Lord could help a poor man like me?"

That alcoholic found God in a manger and we can too. Alcohol abuse may not be the particular area in which you fall short of God's plan. However, we have all fallen short in some way. The good news is that when God became human in Jesus of Nazareth he went all the way down; he was born in a stinking stable that he might rescue you and me out of the depths of our sin and self-centeredness.

MONDAY OF THE THIRD WEEK

A fourth change, which Jesus can bring to our lives, is *a change in companionship*. Matthew correlates the event of Jesus' birth with Isaiah 7:14 which says, "The virgin shall be with child and will give birth to a son, and they will call him Immanuel"—which means, "God with us".

Jesus was born of a virgin, conceived by the power of the Holy Spirit. He is the "with us God". That means we don't have to "go it alone" anymore. One of the greatest needs of human beings is to find an answer to the problem of loneliness.

A school-aged boy in London won first prize for an essay contest. One of the lines from his composition went like this: "I believe so many twins are born into the world today because little children are frightened of entering the world alone!"

The world *is* a frightening place. However, we don't have to go it alone anymore. God wants to walk with us through the struggles. He will be there with us in our joys and in our sorrows once King Jesus has been born in our hearts.

What a contrast there is between Christianity and other religions at this point! For example, in Islam God is always the "above us God". Allah sends—angels, prophets, and books—but he is too holy to come himself. By contrast, in Jesus, God has come near. That makes all the difference.

There was a woman who was having difficulties in her marriage. Finally, she couldn't take it anymore. She walked out on her husband and two children. However, the husband came after her, got her, and lovingly brought her back home. After they reconciled, the wife had this to say about her husband's previous protestations of love: "Before, they were just words ... but then you came."

Jesus took the word of God's love and fleshed it out for us when he was born as a babe in Bethlehem and when he died on a cross for our sin. I imagine that before Jesus was born, God's words seemed to some to be *only* words ... but then he came on our earthly scene in person.

Devotional Thoughts for the Holiday Season

Jesus is the "with us" God, but sometimes I wonder whether we recognize his presence.

Gene Weingarten shared the following story in the Washington Post:

> Joshua Bell emerged from the Metro and positioned himself against a wall beside a trash basket. By most measures, he was nondescript—a youngish white man in jeans, a long-sleeved T-shirt, and a Washington Nationals baseball cap. From a small case, he removed a violin. Placing the open case at his feet, he shrewdly threw in a few dollars and pocket change as seed money and began to play.
>
> For the next 45 minutes, in the D.C. Metro on January 12, 2007, Bell played Mozart and Schubert as over 1,000 people streamed by, most hardly taking notice. If they had paid attention, they might have recognized the young man for the world-renowned violinist he is. They also might have noted the violin he played—a rare Stradivarius worth over $3 million. It was all part of a project arranged by The Washington Post—"an experiment in context, perception, and priorities—as well as an unblinking assessment of public taste. In a banal setting, at an inconvenient time, would beauty transcend?"
>
> Just three days earlier, Joshua Bell sold out Boston Symphony Hall, with ordinary seats going for $100. In the subway, Bell garnered about $32 from the 27 people who stopped long enough to give a donation. [11]

One of the greatest violinists of our time can easily go unnoticed while playing a Stradivarius in a subway station. So too, sadly, Jesus often goes unnoticed, even when he tries to make his presence known in our very midst. We need the alertness that can only come from the Holy Spirit if we are to see Jesus at work in the ordinary situations of our daily lives.

TUESDAY OF THE THIRD WEEK

A fifth change: the birth of Jesus in our lives will lead to *a change in lifestyle*. Jesus' birth led to a lifestyle change for Joseph. Joseph obeyed God's revelation and he took Mary home as his wife. However, Joseph's lifestyle change didn't stop there. He went the extra mile and restrained himself from sexual relations with Mary.

Now why did Joseph do this? He didn't have to. Perhaps he did it so that no one could ever say that Jesus was his son. Perhaps he wanted Jesus' identity as the Son of God to be as clear to others as it was to himself.

What lifestyle change is God calling us to today? What extra mile is he calling us to walk, in order that others might see Jesus in and through our lives?

One thing is certain: if we are to be like Joseph then we need God's gift of purity in our lives. Ephesians 5:3 says, "But among you there must not be even a hint of sexual immorality." That applies to what we say and think as well as to what we do with our bodies. Only Jesus can give us that kind of purity by the power of the Holy Spirit.

That is only one lifestyle change God may be calling us to today. There are many others. However, what it all comes down to is this: HAVE WE ANY ROOM FOR JESUS? Do we have room in our lives for a Jesus who will change our plans, our righteousness, our focus, our companionship, and our very lifestyle? As the old hymn puts it:

> Have you any room for Jesus,
> He who bore your load of sin?
> As He knocks and asks admission,
> Sinner, will you let Him in?
>
> Room for Jesus, King of glory!
> Hasten now, His word obey.
> Swing the heart's door widely open,
> Bid Him enter while you may.

Devotional Thoughts for the Holiday Season

Perhaps Jesus has not yet been born in your life. Maybe you have not yet swung your heart's door widely open to him. However, you can do so today. Bid him enter while you may.

On the other hand, maybe you have invited Jesus into your life, yet you are keeping certain rooms of your life shut and locked against his entry. Perhaps you are keeping the workroom of your life closed to his presence. Maybe you are one sort of person in church and a different sort of person on the job. Perhaps you are keeping your family room shut to him. Maybe you are not allowing his word to govern and guide your family life. Perhaps you are keeping the playroom closed to Christ—the room where you entertain yourself in ways that grieve the Holy Spirit. Have you shut the kitchen door on Jesus? Does he have control of your eating habits? What about the attic—where you keep hurtful memories of things long past, the place where you keep grudges against those who have wronged you?

Jesus wants to come in and clean house. He wants to sweep out the attic, the kitchen, the playroom, the family room, the workroom, and whatever other room there is in your life, and he wants to re-decorate. Will you let him do that beginning today?

Jesus may want to do more than simply clean and redecorate the house that is your life. C. S. Lewis expounds on this in the following manner:

> Imagine yourself as a living house. God comes in to rebuild that house. At first, perhaps, you can understand what He is doing. He is getting the drains right and stopping the leaks in the roof and so on: you knew that those jobs needed doing and so you are not surprised. But presently he starts knocking the house about in a way that hurts abominably and does not seem to make sense. What on earth is He up to? The explanation is that He is building quite a different house from the one you thought of—throwing out a new wing here, putting on an extra floor there, running up towers, making courtyards. You thought you were going to be made into a decent little cottage: but He is building a palace. He intends to come and live in it Himself.[1]

When Jesus comes in, he brings change. None of us like change too much. However, the change Jesus brings is worth it. Do you think Joseph and Mary would have exchanged Jesus for anything or anyone else once he was born to them in the stable? I doubt it. Furthermore, I don't think you will want to trade Jesus for anything or anyone else either.

WEDNESDAY OF THE THIRD WEEK

Christmas is a time of surprises.

There was a woman who was preparing her Christmas cookies. Suddenly there was a knock at her door. She opened the door to find a man, his clothes poor, obviously looking for some Christmas odd jobs. The man asked the woman, "Is there any work I can do for you?"

She asked, "Can you paint?"

"Yes," he said. "I'm a rather good painter."

"Well," she said, "there are two gallons of green paint there, and a brush, and I have a porch out back that needs to be painted. Please do a good job. I'll pay you what the job is worth."

The man said, "Fine. I'll be done quickly."

The woman went back to her cookie making and didn't think much more about the man until there was a knock at the door. Again, she opened the door to find the man standing there; this time he had paint all over his clothes.

She asked, "Did you finish the job?"

"Yes," he answered.

"Did you do a good job?" she queried further.

He responded, "Yes. But lady, there's one thing I'd like to point out to you. That's not a Porsche back there. That's a Mercedes."[12]

Christmas is full of surprises, some of them welcome, some of them unwelcome. As we prepare to celebrate the birth of Christ, it is a good time to think about the God of surprises whom we serve. Our God often surprises us by doing the impossible.

Consider the following story of a barren woman who was enabled to conceive a child by the power of God. Her name was Elizabeth. Her husband's name was Zechariah. The child that God gave them was John the Baptist, the one sent to prepare the way for the Messiah, our Lord Jesus. We read their story in Luke 1:5-25.

> In the time of Herod king of Judea there was a priest named Zechariah,

Devotional Thoughts for the Holiday Season

who belonged to the priestly division of Abijah; his wife Elizabeth was also a descendant of Aaron. Both of them were upright in the sight of God, observing all the Lord's commandments and regulations blamelessly. But they had no children, because Elizabeth was barren; and they were both well along in years.

Once when Zechariah's division was on duty and he was serving as priest before God, he was chosen by lot, according to the custom of the priesthood, to go into the temple of the Lord and burn incense. And when the time for the burning of incense came, all the assembled worshipers were praying outside.

Then an angel of the Lord appeared to him, standing at the right side of the altar of incense. When Zechariah saw him, he was startled and was gripped with fear. But the angel said to him: "Do not be afraid, Zechariah; your prayer has been heard. Your wife Elizabeth will bear you a son, and you are to give him the name John. He will be a joy and delight to you, and many will rejoice because of his birth, for he will be great in the sight of the Lord. He is never to take wine or other fermented drink, and he will be filled with the Holy Spirit even from birth. Many of the people of Israel will he bring back to the Lord their God. And he will go on before the Lord, in the spirit and power of Elijah, to turn the hearts of the fathers to their children and the disobedient to the wisdom of the righteous—to make ready a people prepared for the Lord."

Zechariah asked the angel, "How can I be sure of this? I am an old man and my wife is well along in years."

The angel answered, "I am Gabriel. I stand in the presence of God, and I have been sent to speak to you and to tell you this good news. And now you will be silent and not able to speak until the day this happens, because you did not believe my words, which will come true at their proper time."

Meanwhile, the people were waiting for Zechariah and wondering why he stayed so long in the temple. When he came out, he could not speak to them. They realized he had seen a vision in the temple, for he kept making signs to them but remained unable to speak.

When his time of service was completed, he returned home. After this his wife Elizabeth became pregnant and for five months remained in seclusion. "The Lord has done this for me," she said. "In these days he has shown his favor and taken away my disgrace among the people."

Are you facing an impossible problem? Zechariah and Elizabeth had an impossible problem; they were unable to have children. To be childless, in the Jewish culture of that time, was a great reproach. It was thought that barrenness was a sign of divine punishment. The rabbis said that seven people were excommunicated from God and the list began, "A Jew who has no wife, or a Jew who has a wife and who has no child." Childlessness, in some circles, was thought to be a valid reason for divorce.

Luke tells us that Zechariah and Elizabeth were upright in the sight of God, observing all the Lord's commandments and regulations blamelessly. Thus, we can be sure that Elizabeth's barrenness was not a sign of divine punishment. Yet, when we see good people suffering as Zechariah and Elizabeth suffered we ask, "Why?" As the story unfolds, we see that the reason for Elizabeth's barrenness was so that God would have an opportunity to show forth his power.

Missionary Ian Hall tells the story of a Romanian woman named Cristina Ardeleanu. In March 1992, Cristina was in the hospital with an ectopic pregnancy. Before she learned she was pregnant, the fetus died and began to decompose in her body. Cristina was not expected to live.

Ian and his wife Sheila went to the hospital to pray for Cristina and God healed her. Still, in their attempts to save her life, doctors removed most of her uterus and one ovary. They told her she would never bear a child.

Cristina's strength returned, and soon she was back in church. She and her husband Stefan came for prayer. They asked Ian, "Will you pray that God will give us a child?" Knowing Cristina's diagnosis, the couple was hoping to adopt a child. However, Ian prayed that the couple would be able to give birth to their own child, to the astonishment of everyone gathered in church that day.

In May 1993, Ian was back in Cristina's church in Romania. The pastor announced that a baby would be dedicated and informed Ian that he was to pray for the child. At first, Ian couldn't see anyone in the congregation with a baby. Then from the farthest corner of the church he saw Stefan and Cristina approaching, holding the son born to them six weeks earlier. As with Zechariah and Elizabeth, Stefan and Cristina had received a child by the miraculous work of God.

What is your impossible problem? Is it infertility? Is it cancer? Is it the loss of a job? Is it a problem in your marriage or family? This story does not guarantee that God will always remove infertility, or cancer, or give us the job that we want, or erase marriage and family problems. However, this story does teach us that our God is one who likes to take on impossible situations and show us that all things are possible for him.

THURSDAY OF THE THIRD WEEK

The story of Zechariah and Elizabeth also suggests a second point. That is that prayer is the solution to impossible problems. In verse 13 of Luke 1, Gabriel says to Zechariah, "your prayer has been heard. Your wife Elizabeth will bear you a son." This suggests that Zechariah had prayed about their impossible problem. He had prayed that Elizabeth would bear a child.

Sometimes we are tempted to *not* bring our impossible problems before God. We are afraid that he won't answer or that he can't do anything about our issue. We may think God doesn't care about us. However, this story teaches us that there is no problem too great for God's power and no person too small for his love.

Zechariah may have been tempted to think that he was not important to God. He was only one of twenty thousand priests. The priests were divided into twenty-four sections. Lots were drawn for each duty within each section. Every morning and evening, sacrifice was made for the whole nation. Before the morning sacrifice and after the evening sacrifice, incense was burned on the altar of incense so that the sacrifices might go up to God wrapped, as it were, in an envelope of sweet fragrance. The incense was symbolic of the prayers of God's people. However, with there being as many priests as there were, it was quite possible that many a priest would never have the privilege of burning incense all his life. If the lot did fall on any particular priest to burn incense, that day was the greatest day in all his life.

So here was Zechariah... on the most thrilling day of his existence, entering into God's presence in the temple, presenting the prayers of God's people, and he is met by an angel of the Lord. Furthermore, as we have seen, that angel tells Zechariah: "Your prayer has been heard."

Can you imagine being Zechariah? Can you imagine receiving assurance from an angel, in person, that God has heard your prayers? What an affirmation! Maybe Zechariah *did* matter to God after all.

The Bible assures us that each of us matter to God. He does hear our prayers, if we pray according to his will. (1 John 5:14)

Zechariah was probably less tempted in the future to think that God did not hear his prayers, or to think that he did not matter to God.

Will you dare to pray about your impossible situation and receive in faith God's answer when it comes?

John Newton, the author of that great hymn, *Amazing Grace*, once penned these lines,

> Thou art coming to a King,
> Large petitions with thee bring,
> For His grace and power are such
> None can ever ask too much.

Do you ever dare to pray big prayers to God?

Shortly after Dallas Theological Seminary was founded in 1924, it almost came to the point of bankruptcy. All the creditors were going to foreclose at noon on a particular day. That morning they met for prayer in President Louis Sperry Chafer's office. In that prayer meeting was a man by the name of Harry Ironside. When it was his turn to pray, he prayed in his characteristic manner: "Lord, we know that the cattle on a thousand hills are yours. Please sell some of them and send us the money."

While they were praying, a tall Texan with boots on and an open collar stepped up to the business office and said, "I just sold two carloads of cattle in Ft. Worth. I've been trying to make a business deal but it fell through, and I feel compelled to give the money to the seminary. I don't know if you need it or not, but here's the check!"

The secretary took the check and, knowing how critical things were financially, she went to the president's door and tapped lightly. When she finally got a response, Dr. Chafer took the check out of her hand. It was exactly the amount needed to cover the school's debt. When he looked at the name he recognized the cattleman in Ft. Worth, and turning to Dr. Ironside he said, "Harry, God sold the cattle!"

Are you willing to ask God to solve your impossible problem? Keep in mind, that as Anne Lewis once wrote, "There are four ways God answers prayer: (1) No, not yet; (2) No, I love you too much; (3) Yes, I thought you'd never ask; (4) Yes, and here's more." Be open to the many ways God may answer your prayer. However, don't be surprised when he does answer.

Zechariah was surprised when God answered his prayer. Perhaps he had prayed long ago that Elizabeth would be enabled by God to bear a child. However, when the prayer seemingly went unanswered for so long, maybe Zechariah had given up praying. Now that Elizabeth and he were well along in years, perhaps Zechariah had even given up hoping that they would have a child of their own. Maybe that is why Zechariah asked the angel, "How can

I be sure of this?"

In response to Zechariah's question, the angel struck him dumb. He was unable to speak until after John was born. I'll bet Zechariah learned not to be so surprised at God's answers to prayer after that experience.

FRIDAY OF THE THIRD WEEK

A third thing we can learn from the story of Zechariah and Elizabeth is that God's answer to our impossible problem will bring joy to many.

Gabriel told Zechariah, "He [John] will be a joy and delight to you, and many will rejoice because of his birth."

God gets great glory by working in impossible situations. When God works in your impossible situation it will not only bring *you* joy, but it will bring *others* joy as well.

Can you imagine the giddy joy that Zechariah and Elizabeth must have had, finally bearing a child in old age, after praying for so many years? They must have laughed at God's crazy answer, just as Abraham and Sarah laughed many years before in a similar situation. Furthermore, we read in Luke 1:58 that when Elizabeth's neighbors and relatives heard that the Lord had shown her great mercy, they shared her joy. What a party must have taken place in Elizabeth's town after John was born!

When George Friedrich Handel wrote the *Hallelujah Chorus* his health and his fortunes had reached the lowest possible ebb. His right side had become paralyzed, and all his money was gone. He was heavily in debt and threatened with imprisonment. He was tempted to give up the fight. The odds seemed entirely too great. However, it was then he composed his greatest work—*The Messiah*. [13]

God worked in the midst of Handel's impossible problems, and the work of art that God inspired has brought joy to many. I have heard that each year in Washington, D.C., someone rents a hall, hires an orchestra, and advertises a sing-along production of Handel's *Messiah*. People stand in line to get tickets. The choir numbers in the thousands. People pay for the privilege and joy of singing *The Messiah*.

What is your impossible problem? Are you daring to present that problem before the Lord in prayer, or are you going to deprive yourself and others of the joy of seeing God's answer to your impossible situation?

Devotional Thoughts for the Holiday Season

There was a pastor in Florida who used to have "Count it all joy" parties every now and then. His reason for the parties was based upon James 1:2-3 where it says, "Consider it pure joy, my brothers, whenever you face trials of many kinds, because you know that the testing of your faith develops perseverance."

This pastor so believed in this verse, that when he would face a difficult situation, he would call his friends over to his house. He'd say, "I want you to come over to my house for a party."

His friends would respond, "Is it a birthday party?"

"No," the pastor would say.

"Uh, you got a promotion?" they'd continue.

"No," he'd say.

"What's the situation?" they would finally ask.

"Well," the pastor would say, "I'm going through this incredibly difficult crisis right now, and I'm having a 'Count it all joy' party. We're going to celebrate this difficulty, because I know that this problem is going to bring something of value to my life. I don't know what it is yet, but I want you to come and count it all joy with me."

What a great way to face impossible problems in life! Count it all joy. Present your problems before the Lord in prayer. Get your friends praying and rejoicing with you in advance. Then, when God's solution to your impossible problem comes, you and others will be filled with even greater joy because of our God who makes the impossible possible.

SATURDAY OF THE THIRD WEEK

Late one evening a professor sat at his desk working on the next day's lectures. He shuffled through the papers and mail placed there by his housekeeper. He began to throw them in the wastebasket when one magazine—not even addressed to him but delivered to his office by mistake—caught his attention. It fell open to an article titled: *The Needs of the Congo Mission*.

The professor began reading it idly, but then he was intrigued by these words: "The need is great here. We have no one to work the northern province of Gabon in the central Congo. And it is my prayer as I write this article that God will lay His hand on one—one on whom, already, the Master's eyes have been cast—that he or she shall be called to this place to help us." The professor closed the magazine and wrote in his diary: "My search is over." He gave himself to go to the Congo.

The professor's name was Albert Schweitzer. That little article, hidden in a periodical intended for someone else, was placed "by accident" in Schweitzer's mailbox. "By chance" his housekeeper put the magazine on the professor's desk. "By happenstance" he noticed the title, which seemed to leap out at him. Dr. Schweitzer became one of the great figures of the twentieth century in a humanitarian work nearly unmatched in human history. Was it chance? No, I don't think so. I believe it was the providence of God at work.

By the providence of God, you are reading this book. By the providence of God, you have been born in a certain place, brought up in a certain family, been given certain abilities and certain opportunities. God, in his providence, has chosen you for a special work that only you can do.

God, in his providence, also chose a certain young girl, who lived two thousand years ago, to be the human mother of his Son and our Savior, the Lord Jesus Christ. It is her story that we read from Luke 1:26-56....

> In the sixth month, God sent the angel Gabriel to Nazareth, a town in Galilee, to a virgin pledged to be married to a man named Joseph, a descendant of David. The virgin's name was Mary. The angel went to

her and said, "Greetings, you who are highly favored! The Lord is with you."

Mary was greatly troubled at his words and wondered what kind of greeting this might be. But the angel said to her, "Do not be afraid, Mary, you have found favor with God. You will be with child and give birth to a son, and you are to give him the name Jesus. He will be great and will be called the Son of the Most High. The Lord God will give him the throne of his father David, and he will reign over the house of Jacob forever; his kingdom will never end."

"How will this be," Mary asked the angel, "since I am a virgin?"

The angel answered, "The Holy Spirit will come upon you, and the power of the Most High will overshadow you. So the holy one to be born will be called the Son of God. Even Elizabeth your relative is going to have a child in her old age, and she who was said to be barren is in her sixth month. For nothing is impossible with God."

"I am the Lord's servant," Mary answered. "May it be to me as you have said." Then the angel left her.

I invite you to focus today on verse 37: *"For nothing is impossible with God."* Let us consider the impossible thing that God did in Mary's life.

First, the impossible thing that God did in Mary was *a virgin conception*. It is clear from the verses we have just read that what Luke insists happened to Mary is that God conceived in her womb a child without the aid of a human father.

Now, if you are having trouble believing in the virgin conception of Jesus I ask you to consider these factors:

Factor #1: Luke, who is reporting this story, was a medical doctor (Colossians 4:14). Luke certainly understood how babies are conceived. He knew that a virgin conception was a human impossibility. Yet, he reports it as a fact. Why? Because he obviously believed that, in the case of Jesus' conception, a miracle had taken place.

C. S. Lewis has written, "You will hear people say, 'The early Christians believed that Christ was the son of a virgin, but we know that this is a scientific impossibility.' Such people seem to have an idea that belief in miracles arose at a period when men were so ignorant of the cause of nature that they did not perceive a miracle to be contrary to it. A moment's thought shows this to be nonsense: and the story of the Virgin Birth is a particularly striking example. When St. Joseph discovered that his fiancée was going to have a baby, he not unnaturally decided to repudiate her. Why? Because he knew just as well as any modern gynaecologist that in the ordinary course of nature women do not have babies unless they have lain with men. No doubt the modern gynaecologist knows several things about birth and begetting which St. Joseph did not know. But those things do not concern the main point–that a virgin birth is contrary to the course of nature. And St. Joseph certainly knew *that*... When St. Joseph finally accepted the view that his fiancée's pregnancy was due not to unchastity but to a miracle, he accepted the miracle as something contrary to the known order of nature... Belief in miracles, far from depending on an ignorance of the laws of nature, is only possible in so far as those laws are known."[14]

Factor #2: Luke was a painstaking historian. He tells us that he had researched his story well (Luke 1:1-4). If Luke did not make up this story (and fabrication seems to me highly unlikely in this case) then the only people Luke could have gotten the story of the virgin birth from were members of Jesus' family. Furthermore, Mary seems to be the most likely source for the story. The reason the doctrine of the virgin birth does not appear in the letters of the New Testament was, perhaps, that the other New Testament authors were not familiar with the story. You see, the Gospels were written after most, if not all, of the letters were written. Luke and Matthew record the story of the virgin birth, I believe, because they got the story from another source, one that in some way must have gone back to Jesus' immediate family. I imagine that Mary may not have recognized the importance of the virgin birth for the theology of the church. It was a fact about her son Jesus that she treasured in her own heart, until she was asked about it; then the story came out. At any rate, Luke was a painstaking historian who had done his research and he was a doctor. Personally, I think the only reason he would have reported the story was that he thought it was a historical fact.

Factor #3: the incarnation is a bigger miracle than the virgin birth. God becoming a man is the greatest miracle of all. The virgin birth, as the vehicle for that incarnation, pales as a miracle by comparison to the incarnation. Thus, if you believe in the incarnation then you should have no difficulty believing in the virgin conception of Jesus.

Factor #4: nothing is impossible for the God who created the universe. If there is a God who created the far-flung galaxies of outer space then certainly a virgin conception is not too hard a task for him to accomplish.

C. S. Lewis makes another important point in this regard. He writes, "No woman ever conceived a child, no mare a foal, without Him. But once, and for a special purpose, He dispensed with that long line which is His instrument: once His life-giving finger touched a woman without passing through the ages of interlocked events. Once the great glove of Nature was taken off His hand. His naked hand touched her. There was of course a unique reason for it. That time He was creating not simply a man but the Man who was to be

Himself: was creating Man anew: was beginning, at this divine and human point, the New Creation of all things. The whole soiled and weary universe quivered at this direct injection of essential life—direct, uncontaminated, not drained through all the crowded history of Nature."[15]

A virgin conception is not too hard a feat for a God who causes babies to be conceived every day. The specifics of how God accomplished the virgin conception of Jesus are not part of the story or the church doctrine about it. However, the fact that Matthew and Luke teach that Jesus was born of a virgin is undisputed.

THE FOURTH SUNDAY OF ADVENT

A second thing we need to recognize about this impossible thing that God did in Mary is that it was *not* something Mary asked for. Mary did not ask to be the human mother of the God-Man. I'm sure she had her own dreams and plans for her life with Joseph, her betrothed. However, all of that was interrupted. Her plans were dashed to the ground. Certainly, Mary must have had an inkling of what people would say if she conceived a child out of wedlock. They would say that she had been promiscuous. Joseph might decide not to marry her in the end. Her family might reject her and her father might kick her out of the house. Clearly, this situation was not something to be asked for or desired.

How do you handle God's interruptions in your life? Do you say: Oh, I wish such and such had never happened? Do you brood about it and mournfully ask God, "Why me?" or do you accept God's interruptions in your life submissively and even joyfully?

W. Glyn Evans has written, "God must reserve for Himself the right of the initiative, the right to break into my life without question or explanation. That shattering phone call, that disturbing letter … may indeed be the first stage of God's interruption in my life… Since God does the initiating He must be responsible for the consequences."

We see from this account how Mary reacted to God's interruption in her life. "I am the Lord's servant. May it be to me as you have said." Instead of praying, "Thy will be changed." Mary prayed, "Thy will be done."

Ben Patterson has written, "Medieval artists often portrayed Mary in stained glass windows. Her pane would be the only one with no color on it. Clear glass. All the other windowpanes would filter the light of the sun through their own distinctive designs. Mary was clear, unfiltered. There was nothing of her to affect the light that came through. She could not advance herself and advance the work of God."

I think the medieval artists got it right. Mary was not putting any obstacle in God's way. She allowed God to have his way with her completely in this situation.

Ben Patterson goes on to say, "When we pray, we relinquish in a radical way our so-called sovereignty over the purposes of our lives. We subordinate our plans, schedules and life scenarios to the infinitely wiser and more joyful work of God's hands."

Oswald Chambers once wrote, "If you are a saint, God will continually upset your programme, and if you are wedded to your programme, you will become that most obnoxious creature under heaven, an irritable saint."

For most of 2004, my family and I lived in Ireland with Douglas Gresham, the stepson of C. S. Lewis. I recall Doug telling me one day how his stepfather got into the habit of handling interruptions in his daily routine. If Lewis was working on some important bit of writing and a family member asked him to come and help with something in the kitchen, or some other household chore, Lewis would quietly lay down his pen, get up from his desk, and help his family in whatever way was required. When finished with the task, he would return to his writing desk and continue with his work as though he had never left.

Knowing this about Lewis' personal life, makes these words from Lewis' pen all the more meaningful. Lewis wrote to his friend, Arthur Greeves, on 20 December 1943:

> The great thing, if one can, is to stop regarding all the unpleasant things as interruptions of one's 'own', or 'real' life. The truth is of course that what one calls the interruptions are precisely one's real life—the life God is sending one day by day: what one calls one's 'real life' is a phantom of one's own imagination. This at least is what I see at moments of insight: but it's hard to remember it all the time ... [16]

The example of Mary and the words of Lewis make me pause to ponder: how will I respond the next time God interrupts my life?

MONDAY OF THE FOURTH WEEK

A third thing we need to see about the impossible thing that God did in Mary's life is that it was to be a mixed blessing. Mary was to know a joy like no other; she was to be the mother of the God-Man, the only perfect man who was also fully God. However, she was also to see suffering like no other. Mary was the only person present at Jesus' birth who was also there for his horrific death. As Simeon was to prophesy about Mary's future, "And a sword will pierce your own soul too." (Luke 2:35)

If you knew what was going to happen in your life ahead of time, would you still sign up for the course? If you knew all the future pains as well as all the future joys you were going to experience, would you want to live even for another day?

Perhaps that is why God only reveals to us as much as he knows we can handle. He knows that our knowing all of our future would be too much revelation for us to handle in a moment. Thus, his usual program is to reveal only the next step we need to take. That's what he did in Mary's life and this probably helped her to submit more willingly and joyfully to his will.

The conception of Jesus in Mary's womb was a mixed blessing in her life. All blessings from God in this life are mixed. No circumstance is completely hopeless if we are walking in a relationship with God through Christ. Yet, no situation is perfect because we haven't reached heaven yet.

Eric Liddell, the Olympic runner about whom the movie *Chariots of Fire* was made, once said this, "Circumstances may appear to wreck our lives and God's plans, but God is not helpless among the ruins. Our broken lives are not lost or useless. God's love is still working. He comes in and takes the calamity and uses it victoriously, working out his wonderful plan of love."

Do you remember in *Chariots of Fire* how Eric Liddell refused to run on Sunday because it was the Sabbath? When he is on the boat crossing the English Channel (en route to Paris for the Olympic Games), he finds out that he is scheduled to run in a race on Sunday. He knows what he must do because of his commitment to keep Sunday as a holy day set apart for God. He must decline to run in the race and give up his dream of running in the Olympics. However, God had other plans and arranged for Liddell to trade places with another athlete and run in a different race on a different day.

Eric Liddell went on to serve as a missionary in China and died in a prison camp from a brain tumor. The funeral service for Liddell was crowded; the church could not hold all the people. Thus, many stood outside. Many people came who did not normally attend the church services in the prison camp. For example, a prostitute attended, a woman for whom Eric Liddell had performed chores without asking anything in return.

Was Eric Liddell's life ultimately a great defeat? Did God's cause fail? No, for today the Church is growing in China probably more than anywhere else in the world, in spite of, and perhaps because of government persecution of and restrictions against Christian worship. The testimony of Eric Liddell's life continues.

Eric Liddell's favorite hymn speaks much to us in the midst of the mixed-blessing nature of the Christian life:

> Be still, my soul, the Lord is on thy side
> Bear patiently the cross of grief or pain
> Leave to thy God to order and provide
> In every change He faithful will remain
> Be still, my soul, thy best, thy heavenly Friend
> Through thorny ways leads to a joyful end.

TUESDAY OF THE FOURTH WEEK

And Mary said:
"My soul glorifies the Lord
and my spirit rejoices in God my Savior,
for he has been mindful
of the humble state of his servant.
From now on all generations will call me blessed,
for the Mighty One has done great things for me—
holy is his name.
His mercy extends to those who fear him,
from generation to generation.
He has performed mighty deeds with his arm,
he has scattered those who are proud in their inmost thoughts.
He has brought down rulers from their throne,
but has lifted up the humble.
He has filled the hungry with good things
but has sent the rich away empty.
He has helped his servant Israel
remembering to be merciful
to Abraham and his descendants forever,
even as he said to our fathers." Luke 1:46-55

A fourth thing we can see in Luke 1 is that the impossible thing that God did in Mary was the start of a revolution in a few different but related ways.

First, the conception of Jesus was the beginning of a *moral* revolution. Mary said in her prayer (which we know as the Magnificat): "he has scattered those who are proud in their inmost thoughts."

I believe William Barclay has written very insightfully on this passage of Scripture:

"Christianity is the death of pride. Why? Because if a man sets his life beside that of Christ it tears the last vestiges of pride from him... Christ enables a man to see himself. It is the deathblow to pride. The moral revolution has begun."

Secondly, the virgin conception of Jesus was the beginning of a *social* revolution. Mary said, "He has brought down rulers from their thrones but has lifted up the humble."

Barclay says very pointedly, "Christianity puts an end to the world's labels and prestige ...When we have realized what Christ did for all men, it is no longer possible to speak about a *common* man. The social grades are gone."

Thirdly, the virgin conception of Christ was the beginning of an *economic* revolution. "He has filled the hungry with good things but has sent the rich away empty."

Barclay says, "A non-Christian society is an acquisitive society where each man is out to amass as much as he can get. A Christian society is a society where no man dares to have too much while others have too little, where every man must get only to give away."

A number of years ago I took one of my sons Christmas shopping for the first time in his life, to give him the chance to buy some presents for the rest of the family. The purpose of the trip from my perspective was to give my son the chance to learn that Christmas is about giving as well as receiving. My son had $5 saved from his allowance and we went to Eckerd's Drug Store with his $5 in change in a plastic bag. We found presents for the rest of our family, but you can't buy three presents for $5 even at Eckerd's. I had to chip in about $4 more. Then after we had paid for the presents I remembered that we needed to buy wrapping paper. It was then that my son realized we had spent all of his money on the gifts. He said to me, "Why didn't you tell me I was spending all of my money? I wanted to keep some of it for myself."

I realized my son's teachable moment had arrived. I bent down and asked him, "Do you know what God gave us on Christmas?"

Either he didn't know or didn't want to answer. So I said, "He gave us his Son Jesus and his Son Jesus gave up everything in heaven to come and be born as a human baby and die for us on the cross. Do you think that since Jesus gave up everything for us that you can give up your money to buy presents for others at Christmas time?"

Maybe it was an unfair question for a father to ask his young son. However, it isn't an unfair question for me to ask you. Since God's Son gave up everything to be born as a human baby and die on the cross for your sin, what do you think you might give up for him and for others?

Jesus' coming to earth was the start of a moral, a social and an economic revolution. Since Jesus came to earth and died on the cross for our sins and rose again from the dead he has the power to enable us to live for him and for others rather than for ourselves. Christmas is the season when we give to others because God first gave his Son for us. Furthermore, we can only give to others willingly and joyfully because he first gave his Son for us. That is the impossible work that I hope the Lord will make possible in each of my children's hearts, and in my heart, and in your heart, and everyone's heart, not only during Christmas, but all throughout the year.

WEDNESDAY OF THE FOURTH WEEK

Not far from where I grew up in Southern California there is an observatory called Mount Palomar. In that observatory is one of the largest telescopes in the world. It can look out into the heavens and pick out light so far away that it takes one hour of focusing upon that light for it to make even the faintest impression on a photographic plate. That telescope has a tremendous capacity for focusing upon distant objects. And yet, what that telescope on Mount Palomar can do is nothing compared to the way in which God focused himself in the Word made flesh, Jesus of Nazareth, the human baby whose birth we celebrate at Christmas.

J. B. Phillips once wrote, "Every day science discovers more and more of the complex wisdom of God. Anyone who uses his mind has a much bigger idea of God than our grandfathers, or even our fathers ever had. Yet God has been here on the planet in person. What we are celebrating ... is not the feast of jolly old Father Christmas or good King Wenceslaus, or a beautiful fairy-tale. We are celebrating the visit of God."

That is the amazing, impossible thing that God did two thousand years ago: he became a human being. It is the birth of the God-Man Jesus Christ that we read about in Luke 2:1-7...

> In those days Caesar Augustus issued a decree that a census should be taken of the entire Roman world. (This was the first census that took place while Quirinius was governor of Syria.) And everyone went to his own town to register.
>
> So Joseph also went up from the town of Nazareth in Galilee to Judea, to Bethlehem the town of David, because he belonged to the house and line of David. He went there to register with Mary, who was pledged to be married to him and was expecting a child. While they were there, the time came for the baby to be born, and she gave birth to her firstborn, a son. She wrapped him in cloths and placed him in a manger, because there was no room for them in the inn.

Devotional Thoughts for the Holiday Season

There are at least three amazing things about Jesus' birth in this passage. First, *the Prince of Peace was born during the Pax Romana.*

Luke tells us that Jesus was born in the days when Caesar Augustus issued a decree that a census should be taken of the entire Roman world. This statement anchors Jesus' birth firmly in history.

Caesar Augustus ushered in the Pax Romana, or Roman peace. James Boice once wrote, "Prior to the reign of Augustus the empire had been in great turmoil. There had been the advance of Julius Caesar over the Rubicon, which led to the death of the Republic and in time to Caesar's own death by assassination. That was followed by the civil wars in which Antony and Octavius defeated Brutus and Cassius. Then there was war between Antony and the quickly ascending Augustus. In all there were twenty years of turmoil, and it was only at the end of that period that Augustus, now the sole ruler of the empire, established peace. Moreover, it was not only in civil war that Augustus proved victorious. He also conducted wars on the various borders of the empire against invaders and on the seas against pirates. He established the Pax Romana."

The reason I say that the Prince of Peace being born during the Pax Romana is amazing is because it was the best time for Jesus to be born. The Pax Romana is significant to the birth of Christianity because it made possible the spread of the Gospel of Jesus Christ throughout the whole Roman Empire. Under the Pax Romana, instead of fighting wars, roads were built across the empire and it was safe to travel. This offered a unique opportunity in the ancient world for the birth and explosion of Christianity.

Because of the Pax Romana in the Eastern Mediterranean, Augustus was hailed as a savior and a god. A tribute to Augustus from that time reads: the birthday "of the god has marked the beginning of the good news through him for the world."

N. T. Wright has written, "But the point Luke is making is clear. The birth of this little boy is the beginning of a confrontation between the kingdom of God—in all its apparent weakness, insignificance and vulnerability—and the kingdoms of the world. Augustus never heard of Jesus of Nazareth. But within a century or so his successors in Rome had not only heard of him; they were taking steps to obliterate his followers. Within just over three centuries the Emperor himself became a Christian. When you see the manger on a card, or in a church, don't stop at the crib. See what it's pointing to. It is pointing to the explosive truth that the baby lying there is already being spoken of as the true king of the world."

The Bible tells us that the real bearer of peace is not Caesar Augustus but Jesus. The Prince of Peace, who is Jesus, is the only one who can bring lasting peace to our troubled world and to our disturbed souls.

Open Before Christmas

A friend visited an elderly woman badly crippled by arthritis. When asked, "Do you suffer much?" she responded, "Yes, but there is no nail here," and she pointed to her hand. "He had the nails, I have the peace." She pointed to her head. "There are no thorns here. He had the thorns, I have the peace." She touched her side. "There is no spear here. He had the spear, I have the peace."

That is what God becoming human means for us. He became a human being, in part, so that he might die on a cross for our sins. We give him our sins and, in exchange, he gives us his peace that reigns in our souls. The problem is that we often want peace without the Prince of Peace, and that is not possible.

THURSDAY OF THE FOURTH WEEK

The second amazing thing we see in Luke 2 about the birth of Christ is that Jesus was born in Bethlehem. This may not seem that unusual to those of us who are overly familiar with the story of the birth of Christ. However, let us think about this for a moment.

God used the actions of human rulers to insure that his Son would be born in Bethlehem. If it had not been for Caesar Augustus issuing his decree and Quirinius conducting the census, Joseph and Mary would probably have stayed in Nazareth and Jesus would have been born there. However, as Micah indicates, it was God's plan all along that his Son should be born in Bethlehem and this was probably the case for at least two reasons. First, Bethlehem was the town of David. Thus, by causing Jesus to be born in Bethlehem God was telling us that Jesus was and is the long-awaited Messiah. Secondly, as we have already seen, the name Bethlehem means "House of Bread." Jesus was and is the Bread of Life as he later claimed in John 6:35, "I am the bread of life. He who comes to me will never go hungry, and he who believes in me will never be thirsty."

Read the label on the last loaf of bread you bought. More than likely you will discover that it has been filled with alien vitamins and preservatives. Bread is not the simple thing it once was. However, no one can improve on the Bread of Life; it is unique. You can make physical bread from wheat, rye, rice, barley, corn, and even from potatoes. The best bread for the soul can come only from one source: Jesus Christ.

A common expression to describe extreme conditions of poverty is to say that a person is on a diet of bread and water. Prisoners in solitary confinement have sometimes been given nothing more than that. Monks in their ascetic zeal have sometimes limited their diet to bread and water. Bread and water may not sound very nourishing. However, spiritual bread and water is all we need to live a full, healthy spiritual life. Jesus is the bread of life; he also said that he is the water of life. He is all that we need.

Open Before Christmas

Bible teacher Harry Ironside used to tell the story of an old woman who was in distress because of her deep poverty. She was living in a little garret in London and was afraid that one day the police would come and arrest her because of her debts. It happened that a Christian minister heard of her situation and raised money to pay off her creditors. Then, with the receipt for the debt in his pocket and with provision for her present needs, he went to find her. The neighbors knew her only by the name "Old Betty." Thus, when he got to the building where she lived, the minister asked, "Can you tell me where Old Betty lives?"

He was told to go up the stairs to a certain room. He went to the door and knocked. He waited, but there was no answer. He knocked again. No answer. He called, "Betty, are you in there?" Nothing.

At last, he went back down the stairs and started to leave. However, as he left, her neighbors asked him, "Did you find her?"

"No," he answered. "She is not in."

"Oh, she's in, all right. She's just not letting you in. She's afraid you are one of her creditors, and she is just not opening the door."

When he heard this, the minister went back up the stairs to the room and called out, "Betty, let me in! I'm the minister, and I've come to see you."

"Oh," came the voice from inside. "I thought you were the police, and I was afraid to open the door." When the door finally opened, the minister told her that friends had raised money to cancel her debt, had paid it, and had sent him to tell her, give her the receipt, and present her with an additional amount for her current needs. Betty was overwhelmed and embarrassed. "Just think," she said, "I locked and bolted the door against you. I was afraid to let you in."

You and I are like Betty. The minister is like Christ. We are often afraid to open our door to him. Yet, he has undertaken to cancel the debt of our sin by his own death, and he has come to provide for us now and for always. He is our best friend, yet we have kept him out. Furthermore, we often continue to keep him out until the compulsion of his grace moves us to open the door to him and admit him into the deep recesses of our lives.

Jesus said in Revelation 3:20, "Here I am! I stand at the door and knock. If anyone hears my voice and opens the door, I will come in and eat with him, and he with me."

Jesus Christ wants to have a relationship with you. He came to this earth, was born as a human being, died on the cross for your sins, and rose again from the dead so that you could know his peace and so that you could be spiritually nourished to the full. However, you have to let him in.

FRIDAY OF THE FOURTH WEEK

A third amazing thing we see in Luke 2 about Jesus' birth is that *there was no room in the inn for the one who makes room for us in heaven.*

Caesar had no room for Jesus. James Boice once wrote, "There was no room for Him in the palaces of this world's kings. Caesar would not make room. The idea of the great Augustus making room for the humble carpenter from Nazareth and his pregnant companion Mary is preposterous."

Quirinius had no room for Jesus. He, like Caesar, probably had no knowledge even of Christ's existence. Charles Spurgeon once wrote: "... seldom is there room for Christ in palaces! How could the kings of earth receive the Lord? He is the Prince of Peace, and they delight in war! He breaks their bows and cuts their spears asunder; he burneth their war-chariots in the fire. How could kings accept the humble Savior? They love grandeur and pomp, and he is all simplicity and meekness. He is a carpenter's son, and the fisherman's companion. How can princes find room for the new-born monarch? Why he teaches us to do to others as we would that they should do to us, and this is a thing which kings would find very hard to reconcile with the knavish tricks of politics and the grasping designs of ambition."

The rich families of Bethlehem made no room for Jesus. Joseph Bayly once wrote the following Psalm for Christmas:

> Lord we blame
> the innkeeper
> for only giving you the stable
> when his inn was full
> but what about
> all the others
> who lived in Bethlehem
> that night
> when you were born.

> Why were
> all their houses
> that weren't full
> of guests
> fast closed
> against the one
> who contained you?
> God bless
> our little homes
> this Christmastime
> make them
> big enough
> to welcome you
> contained in those
> for whom the world
> has no room
> except
> a cold and lonely
> Christmas day.

The poor made no room for Jesus either. We often think rich people were staying in the inn in Bethlehem, but they were not. Only the poor would stay in an inn in that time. The rich would stay in homes.

One Christmas season a teacher was teaching a group of first graders in public school. They were studying Christmas customs from around the world. Thus, this particular teacher took the opportunity to tell the class the story of Mary and Joseph and the baby Jesus. She explained how Mary and Joseph had gone to Bethlehem to pay taxes. It was time for the baby Jesus to be born and they needed somewhere to spend the night. The teacher told her students that when they went to the inn, there were no empty rooms. She compared the inn to a modern-day hotel or motel. She was leading up to the stable when she asked, "What do you suppose they had behind the inn?"

One little boy, who had been listening intently, began to frantically wave his hand. His face was alight with knowledge. He said, "A swimming pool!"

Well, they didn't have a swimming pool behind the inn in Bethlehem because it was an inn for poor people, and none of them gave up their room for Mary and Joseph. None of them made room for the God-Man to be born in their midst.

Of course, we all know that the innkeeper had no room for Jesus. However, why did he have such difficulty in making room for this couple that obviously needed a clean place for their baby to be born? Author Frederick

Devotional Thoughts for the Holiday Season

Buechner puts the following speech on the lips of the innkeeper,

> I speak to you as men of the world, not as idealists but as realists. Do you know what it is like to run an inn–to run a business, a family, to run anything in this world for that matter, even your own life? It is like being lost in a forest of a million trees, and each tree is a thing to be done. Is there fresh linen on all the beds? Did the children put on their coats before they went out? Has the letter been written, the book read? Is there money enough left in the bank? Today we have food in our bellies and clothes on our backs, but what can we do to make sure that we will have them still tomorrow? A million trees. A million things. Until finally we have eyes for nothing else, and whatever we see turns into a thing... Of course I remember very well the evening they arrived. I was working on my accounts and looked up just in time to see the woman coming through the door... I did not lie about there being no room left—there really was none—though perhaps if there had been a room, I might have lied... Later that night, when the baby came, I was not there. I was lost in the forest somewhere, the unenchanted forest of a million trees... But this I do know. My own true love. All your life long, you wait for your own true love to come—we all of us do—our destiny, our joy, our heart's desire. So how am I to say it, gentlemen? When he came, I missed him.

The only place where there was room for Jesus was in a manger, a feeding trough for animals. Prince Philip, the husband of Queen Elizabeth II, was born a Greek prince, though there is no Greek blood in his veins. He is of German and Danish ancestry. As a baby, he was smuggled out of Greece in a crate made from an orange box. A crate hardly befits a prince, and a manger hardly befits the infant King of Kings. How amazing that the one who was really bigger than the whole universe was contained for a time in a little, lowly manger.

How amazing also, that though there was no room for Jesus, except in a manger, he is making room for us in heaven. In John 14:2 we read the words of Jesus, "In my Father's house are many rooms; if it were not so, I would have told you. I am going there to prepare a place for you." He took our place in a manger and on a cross where he paid for our sins so that we could share his place in heaven. How stunning.

However, if we want to share his place in heaven, then we have to make room for him in our hearts and lives here and now.

CHRISTMAS EVE

Max Lucado has written in *The Applause of Heaven*, "An ordinary night with ordinary sheep and ordinary shepherds. And were it not for a God who loves to hook an 'extra' on the front of the ordinary, the night would have gone unnoticed. The sheep would have been forgotten, and the shepherds would have slept the night away.

But God dances amidst the common. And that night he did a waltz.

The black sky exploded with brightness... Sheep that had been silent became a chorus of curiosity. One minute the shepherd was dead asleep, the next he was rubbing his eyes and staring into the face of an alien.

The night was ordinary no more.

The angel came in the night because that is when lights are best seen and that is when they are most needed. God comes into the common for the same reason.

It is from the story of these common shepherds that I believe we learn best how to celebrate Christmas. Let's see what the shepherd's story has to teach us.

And there were shepherds living out in the fields nearby, keeping watch over their flocks at night. An angel of the Lord appeared to them, and the glory of the Lord shone around them, and they were terrified. But the angel said to them, "Do not be afraid. I bring you good news of great joy that will be for all the people. Today in the town of David a Savior has been born to you; he is Christ the Lord. This will be a sign to you: You will find a baby wrapped in cloths and lying in a manger."

Suddenly a great company of the heavenly host appeared with the angel, praising God and saying,

"Glory to God in the highest, and on earth peace to men on whom his favor rests."

Devotional Thoughts for the Holiday Season

> When the angels had left them and gone into heaven, the shepherds said to one another, "Let's go to Bethlehem and see this thing that has happened, which the Lord has told us about."
>
> So they hurried off and found Mary and Joseph, and the baby, who was lying in the manger. When they had seen him, they spread the word concerning what had been told them about this child, and all who heard it were amazed at what the shepherds said to them. But Mary treasured up all these things and pondered them in her heart. The shepherds returned, glorifying and praising God for all the things they had heard and seen, which were just as they had been told.
>
> (Luke 2:8-20)

What can we learn from the shepherds about celebrating Christmas? First, if we are to celebrate Christmas as the shepherds did, we must **hear the Good News.** The angel said to the shepherds, "I bring you good news of great joy that will be for all the people. Today in the town of David a Savior has been born to you; he is Christ the Lord."

The good news we need to hear is that a savior has been born for us and he is Christ the Lord. How is Jesus a savior? What was he born to save us from?

C. S. Lewis answers those questions by telling a story:

> Did you ever think, when you were a child, what fun it would be if your toys could come to life? Well suppose you could really have brought them to life. Imagine turning a tin soldier into a real little man. It would involve turning the tin into flesh. And suppose the tin soldier did not like it. He is not interested in flesh; all he sees is that the tin is being spoiled. He thinks you are killing him. He will do everything he can do to prevent you. He will not be made into a man if he can help it.
>
> What you would have done about that tin soldier I do not know. But what God did about us was this. The Second Person in God, the Son, became human Himself: was born into the world as an actual man—a real man of a particular height, with hair of a particular color, speaking a particular language, weighing so many stone. The Eternal Being, who knows everything and who created the whole universe, became not only a man but (before that) a baby, and before that a fetus inside a Woman's body. If you want to get the hang of it, think how you would like to become a slug or a crab.
>
> The result of this was that you now had one man who really was what all men were intended to be: one man in whom created life, derived from his Mother, allowed itself to be completely and perfectly turned into the begotten life. The natural human creature in Him was taken up fully into the divine Son. Thus in one instance humanity had, so

to speak, arrived: had passed into the life of Christ. And because the whole difficulty for us is that the natural life has to be, in a sense, 'killed,' He chose an earthly career which involved the killing of His human desires at every turn—poverty, misunderstanding from His own family, betrayal by one of His intimate friends, being jeered at and manhandled by the Police, and execution by torture. And then, after being thus killed—killed every day in a sense—the human creature in Him, because it was united to the divine Son, came to life again. The Man in Christ rose again: not only the God. That is the whole point. For the first time we saw a real man. One tin soldier—real tin, just like the rest—had come fully and splendidly alive.[17]

That's the good news of the Gospel. One tin soldier has come fully, splendidly alive, and we can share in that new life if we get close enough to him to catch his "good infection" as C. S. Lewis calls it.

CHRISTMAS DAY

The second thing we need to do in order to celebrate Christmas like the shepherds is to **go and see.** We read that, "When the angels had left them and gone into heaven, the shepherds said to one another, 'Let's **go** to Bethlehem and **see** this thing that has happened, which the Lord has told us about.'" (Luke 2:15)

How can we go and see the newborn Christ child? How can we get close enough to him to catch his "good infection", the infection of righteousness?

There is a Russian proverb: "He who has this disease called Jesus will never be cured." However, how do we get close to him to catch this "disease"? Jesus is not being born again every year in Bethlehem like he was born that first Christmas.

I believe one way we can get close to Jesus today is by reading his story in the Bible which tells of his birth, his life, his death for our sins, his resurrection from the dead, and his instructions for us on how to live for him. One way we can communicate with Jesus is, not by traveling to Bethlehem and talking to the little baby in the manger, but by speaking to Jesus in heaven through prayer.

The thing is, if we want to go and see God in Christ, we better be ready for the kind of God we are going to meet. H.G. Wells, who was no friend of the church, wrote an interesting story years ago in the *New Yorker*. He told a story about a clergyman who was the kind of man who was always saying pious things to people. When people in trouble came to him with their problems, he would say things like, "Have you prayed about that?" This clergyman found that if he said that, in just the right way, it would settle things for people.

The clergyman didn't pray much himself. After all, his life was going along just fine. However, one day he found himself overwhelmed by problems. It occurred to him that he ought to take some of his own advice. Thus, one Saturday afternoon he entered the church, he went to the front and knelt on the crimson rug. He folded his hands before the altar and he began to pray, "O God…"

Suddenly there was a voice. It was crisp, businesslike. The voice said, "Well, what is it?"

The next day when the worshipers came to Sunday services, they found their pastor sprawled face down on the crimson carpet. When they turned him over, they discovered he was dead. Lines of horror were etched upon his face.

I think what H.G. Wells was saying in that story is simply this: there are people who talk a lot about God who would be scared to death if they saw him face to face.

If we are going to go and see God in Christ, by looking into the Bible and by praying, we had better be prepared for the God we are going to meet. He will not be the gentle Jesus, meek and mild of the cradle. For the Christ of the cradle has gone to the cross for our sins and he now wears a crown in heaven. He is the Lord of glory. He is an awesome God. However, he is also our merciful Savior who longs to hear a word from us, and aches to reveal his love.

THE SECOND DAY OF CHRISTMAS

A third thing we can do to celebrate Christmas like the shepherds is to *spread the word*. We read about the shepherds that, "When they had seen him, they spread the word concerning what had been told them about this child." (Luke 2:17)

How could the shepherds have kept from spreading the word about the baby Jesus? They had just seen God incarnate lying in a manger. They had heard the angel hosts of heaven announcing the Savior's birth. In short, they had just witnessed the most stupendous thing ever to happen in human history, and perhaps, in the history of the universe.

There was a little boy in his first Christmas pageant. He was five years old. He was one of the shepherds—you know, the ones that wear their bathrobes and their sandals and carry cardboard crooks—not a lead shepherd, just a common shepherd standing in the back. However, when it came time for the baby Jesus to be born, he crowded around to the front so that he could see. Then, having seen, he stepped to the footlights and, looking out, cried out to his parents, "Mommy! Daddy! Mary had her baby, and it's a boy!"

I think that little five-year-old bath-robed shepherd caught the enthusiasm of those first shepherds in Bethlehem. It is the same enthusiasm we need to catch that will propel us to share the good news of Christ with others.

That leads to a fourth thing we need to do to celebrate Christmas in the best way, and that is to *be amazed*. We read that all who heard the shepherd's report were amazed at what the shepherds said to them. (Luke 2:18)

When it comes to Christmas, we need to recover the wonder of children. It is not that their wonder is a spiritual wonder, necessarily, but children's wonder and amazement at Christmas gives us a picture of the wonder and amazement we ought to have toward the Lord.

One Christmas when our boys were younger it was such a joy to see Joshua crawling and reaching out for the ornaments on the lowest branches of our Christmas tree. Oh yes, it meant more work for Mom and Dad to keep the tree in tact. However, it was worth it, I think, to see the wonder in his eyes.

Then there was Jonathan's amazement at Santa Claus. At that point in time he still didn't like to get too close to Santa, but he loved to stare in wonder at him from afar.

There was James' fascination with presents that kept building, up and up. Every day he would check to see if there was another present for him under the tree. On some evenings, he would lie right next to the tree and stare at those presents in wonder.

We need to become more like our children when it comes to the true meaning of Christmas. We should be reaching out and trying to grasp a hold of it, though the meaning of Christmas, the incarnation, is too big for us to comprehend. We should look in wonder at the chief character of Christmas, not Santa Claus, but the Lord Jesus Christ, and marvel at his person and his works. We should revel in the gift that God has given to us through Christmas, the gift of eternal life, and we should wait with longing for the full unwrapping of that gift that will only come with Christ's return to earth.

THE THIRD DAY OF CHRISTMAS

A fifth thing we can do to celebrate Christmas in the best way is to ***treasure and ponder these things in our hearts.*** When Mary heard the shepherd's story that's what she did. (Luke 2:19)

In one *Dennis the Menace* comic strip Dennis asks his father, "Why can't Christmas ever go into overtime?"

Christmas *can* go into overtime as we treasure and ponder the truth of the Incarnation all year round.

How do we do that? First, we remember the event of God becoming a man.

Second, we can remember the moment when this event became something real and personal to us. We remember when we first realized that Jesus was born for us, to save us from our sin. That will stir up our affections towards Christ.

Third, we need to think about these things and allow God to teach us more about his wonderful work. This involves reading Scripture and reading other Christian writings that deal with the Incarnation.

This leads to a final thing I think we can do to celebrate Christmas the way the shepherds did, that is to ***glorify and praise God.*** We read: "The shepherds returned, glorifying and praising God for all the things they had heard and seen, which were just as they had been told." (Luke 2:20)

To glorify someone means to put the spotlight on him or her—to acknowledge his or her true worth. To glorify God is, at least in part, to worship him by words. It is to reflect back to him accurately who he is.

For example, the moon reflects the light of the sun. The moon has no light of its own. When there is a full moon it shines so brightly and even lights up the earth, but only because it is reflecting the light of the sun. In the same way, we have no glory of our own. The only light we have, spiritually speaking, is the light of Christ. We are called to reflect his light, to accurately reflect back to him who he is. That is what we ought to live for: to bask in his radiance, to reflect it, and bring it to the world around us, not for our own sake, but for Christ's sake.

One way that we can glorify and praise God is through singing, and the best songs to sing are the ones that most accurately reflect *who* God is and *what* he has done for us. Singing praise to God is not just something to do in church. It is something we can do while sitting at home, driving in the car, or walking through the woods.

Isn't it amazing how the joy of the Christmas season causes people to sing carols in all sorts of places? People go singing from house to house. They stroll through malls humming Christmas tunes while they shop.

The joy of the Savior need not be confined to the Christmas season. If we would but ponder the truth of Christ all year round then we would be so filled with his presence that it would naturally overflow into praise seven days a week.

What this all comes down to is the fact that **Christmas demands a response.** The event of Christmas, God becoming human, is not something that anyone can afford to ignore.

Larry Walters was a 33-year-old man who decided he wanted to see his neighborhood from a new perspective. He went down to the local army surplus store one morning and bought forty-five used weather balloons. That afternoon he strapped himself into a lawn chair, to which several of his friends tied the now helium-filled balloons. He took along a six-pack of beer, a peanut-butter-and-jelly sandwich, and a BB gun, figuring he could shoot the balloons one at a time when he was ready to land.

Walters, who assumed the balloons would lift him about one hundred feet in the air, was caught off guard when the chair soared more than eleven thousand feet into the sky—smack into the middle of the air traffic pattern of Los Angeles International Airport. Too frightened to shoot any of the balloons, he stayed airborne for more than two hours, forcing the airport to shut down its runways for much of the afternoon, causing long delays in flights from across the country.

Soon after he was safely grounded and cited by the police, reporters asked Larry three questions and got three simple answers:

"Were you scared?"

"Yes."

"Would you do it again?"

"No."

"Why did you do it?"

"Because," he said, "you can't just sit there."

When it comes to the good news of Christmas you can't just sit there. Christmas demands a response. What is your response?

THE FOURTH DAY OF CHRISTMAS

In recent days, we have looked at how God did the impossible by causing a barren woman, Elizabeth, to conceive a baby. We have seen God doing the impossible again in the life of Mary, a virgin, by causing her to conceive Jesus in her womb. We have examined the grand miracle of the Incarnation, God becoming a human being. And now we look at a somewhat minor miracle: how God moved two elderly people, Simeon and Anna, to be in the right place (the Temple in Jerusalem) at the right time (when the baby Jesus was being presented) in order that they could see God's salvation and talk about it to others.

Around the time of Jesus' birth, there was heightened messianic expectation. Many people in Israel were hoping and expecting the Messiah to come in their lifetime. Many were hoping that the Messiah would come and deliver them from Roman rule. Some sought to bring this about through revolution. However, there were others, known as the Quiet in the Land; they had no dreams of violence, of power grabbing, or armies with banners. These quiet people believed in a life of constant prayer and watchfulness until the Messiah should come. All their lives they waited calmly and patiently for God to send this Messiah to Israel. Simeon and Anna were among these Quiet People of the Land.

I think that in many ways the days of Simeon and Anna are similar to our own. Simeon and Anna lived on the verge of a new era in world history. Today we are poised on the brink of a new year with perennial expectation for positive change and, on the other hand, concern for possible world catastrophe of one sort or another. How are we to enter the coming year in a godly fashion? The lives of Simeon and Anna provide an answer to that question. Let's look at their answer together in Luke 2:21-40....

> On the eighth day, when it was time to circumcise him, he was named Jesus, the name the angel had given him before he had been conceived.
>
> When the time of their purification according to the Law of Moses had been completed, Joseph and Mary took him to Jerusalem to

present him to the Lord (as it is written in the Law of the Lord, "Every firstborn male is to be consecrated to the Lord"), and to offer a sacrifice in keeping with what is said in the Law of the Lord: "a pair of doves or two young pigeons."

Now there was a man in Jerusalem called Simeon, who was righteous and devout. He was waiting for the consolation of Israel, and the Holy Spirit was upon him. It had been revealed to him by the Holy Spirit that he would not die before he had seen the Lord's Christ. Moved by the Spirit, he went into the temple courts. When the parents brought in the child Jesus to do for him what the custom of the Law required, Simeon took him in his arms and praised God, saying:

> "Sovereign Lord, as you have promised,
> you now dismiss your servant in peace.
> For my eyes have seen your salvation,
> which you have prepared in the sight of all people,
> a light for revelation to the Gentiles
> and for glory to your people Israel."

The child's father and mother marveled at what was said about him. Then Simeon blessed them and said to Mary, his mother: "This child is destined to cause the falling and rising of many in Israel, and to be a sign that will be spoken against, so that the thoughts of many hearts will be revealed. And a sword will pierce your own soul too."

There was also a prophetess, Anna, the daughter of Phanuel, of the tribe of Asher. She was very old; she had lived with her husband seven years after her marriage, and then was a widow until she was eighty-four. She never left the temple but worshiped night and day, fasting and praying. Coming up to them at that very moment, she gave thanks to God and spoke about the child to all who were looking forward to the redemption of Jerusalem.

When Joseph and Mary had done everything required by the Law of the Lord, they returned to Galilee to their own town of Nazareth. And the child grew and became strong; he was filled with wisdom, and the grace of God was upon him.

The first thing I think we can learn from Simeon about how to enter a new year is, simply, *to wait*. We read of Simeon in verse 25 that: "He was *waiting* for the consolation of Israel, and the Holy Spirit was upon him."

We gather from the fact that Simeon prayed to the Lord, "You may now dismiss your servant in peace," that he was an old man. He had been waiting all his life for the Messiah to come. The coming of the Messiah is what would bring consolation, or comfort, to Israel, God's people.

Devotional Thoughts for the Holiday Season

Ben Patterson has written, "Waiting is not just the thing we have to do until we get what we hope for. Waiting is part of the process of becoming what we hope for."

Ben illustrates this truth using the following story:

> When my first son was but four years old, my wife and I took him to Disneyland for the first time. When I enter the gates of the Magic Kingdom, something magic happens to me—I regress emotionally, about thirty years. When we arrived, the first thing I wanted to do, as I rushed through the park, practically dragging my son by the hand, was to get in line for my favorite ride—Space Mountain, a roller coaster of a ride with a spaceship motif and lots of speed and wild turns. This was to be Danny's first exposure to an amusement park ride. The Disney people must have a rationale for the way they organize the long lines for their rides—a 'queuing theory' for the wait. I think they must set it up so you can hear, as you wait, the screams of those already on the ride. Listening to all that, by the time you get to the ride you are so agitated yourself that the ride takes on even greater, more terrifying psychological proportions. As we got closer, it finally began to dawn on me that this ride might not be the best introduction of my son to the wonders of amusement parks. Remembering how sensitive his stomach can be, I began to mentally calculate how long it had been since he had eaten breakfast. I asked him, 'Danny, are you sure you want to ride this thing?' (As though it had been his idea, not mine!) He looked up at me with trusting eyes and said, 'Yes, Daddy.' Thus we got into our little spaceship, him completely at ease with his father's judgment. Moments later, as the spaceship twisted and lurched madly over the track at high speed, the knuckles on his chubby little hands grew white as they gripped the bar across our lap, and his little body became one with mine. In a desperate effort to reassure him and calm his stomach, I began to shout frantically, 'Isn't this fun! Isn't this fun!' When the ride was over, and we walked shakily back to his concerned mother, I asked him if he ever wanted to do it again. He said, 'Not just now, Daddy.' The ride was wild and frightening, but—and here's the point of this little story—*while we rode together, Danny stayed closer to me than he ever had, or has since.* And he listened to my voice better than he ever does. The paradoxical journey of waiting, moving from the known to the unknown, the seen to the unseen of God's future, will have some terrifying moments in it. Ease and predictability are not among God's promises. But as we wait, as we journey, we will find ourselves clinging to God as never before, and listening for his voice as if our life depended on it! That in itself, makes the waiting worth the while.

THE FIFTH DAY OF CHRISTMAS

A second thing closely associated with waiting is **watching.** The word *waiting* in Luke 2:25 can also mean *to look for* or *expect*. The same word is used in verse 38 where Luke says that Anna spoke about Jesus to all who were *looking forward* to the redemption of Jerusalem.

As we have already seen, in the time of Simeon and Anna there was a heightened expectation for the Messiah to come. Yet, different groups of people in Israel were looking for different things. The Zealots, like Judas Iscariot, were looking for a revolutionary Messiah to deliver them from the political power of Rome and set up a worldly kingdom of God. The Pharisees, who were the strict religionists of their day, were looking for a rule-keeping Messiah. The Essenes, who were an ascetic community of monks, were looking for an ascetic Messiah who would practice fasting and the like. They did not expect the Messiah to be like Jesus—eating, drinking and attending parties. Then there were the Sadducees, the religious liberals of the day. They weren't looking for anything. They didn't expect the Messiah to literally be a person who would come to earth and deliver them as the Hebrew Scriptures had prophesied. They were probably tempted to spiritualize all the teachings of the Scriptures about the Messiah.

In the midst of this scene, Simeon and Anna recognized the Messiah in a little baby in the Temple in Jerusalem. How were they able to do that?

I think they were able to recognize the Messiah when he came because they were both walking in a close relationship with God. They were "looking out for", they were watching and listening for, the Messiah that God had promised. They were sensitive to the nudges of the Holy Spirit. Thus, they sensed the Spirit telling them that this baby was indeed the Messiah. Furthermore, they didn't question God when he told them who the Messiah really was.

In the same way, I believe the Lord wants us as Christians, as we begin a new year, and all the time really, to be watching diligently for the second coming of the Messiah, our Lord Jesus.

Devotional Thoughts for the Holiday Season

Jesus said this about his second coming,

> No one knows about that day or hour, not even the angels in heaven, nor the Son, but only the Father. Be on guard! Be alert! You do not know when that time will come. It's like a man going away: He leaves his house and puts his servants in charge, each with his assigned task, and tells the one at the door to keep watch.
>
> Therefore keep watch because you do not know when the owner of the house will come back–whether in the evening, or at midnight, or when the rooster crows, or at dawn. If he comes suddenly, do not let him find you sleeping. What I say to you, I say to everyone: 'Watch!' (Mark 13:32-37)

One Christmas there was a little boy who desperately wanted a wristwatch. The boy kept reminding his parents of what he wanted for Christmas, as only little boys can do. Finally, the parents were tired of being reminded so they told their son, "If you mention that present one more time, you will be sure *not* to get it." That made the little boy quiet down quick.

At last, Christmas was approaching, just a few days away. The family had a special ritual at the dinner table. Each person would pray and each child could read a Scripture passage of his or her choice. The boy's turn came to pick the Scripture passage and so he picked Mark 13:37, reading it with great enthusiasm: "What I say to you, I say to everyone: 'Watch!'"

We need to have the same enthusiasm and perseverance of that boy when it comes to "watching" for Jesus' coming.

"Watch" was a very important word in Jesus' discourse about his Second Coming. He tells us that none of us can know the future. We do not know when he is going to return to earth. He tells us that he doesn't even know, only the Father knows. He could return sometime in the coming year, or he could return before you finish reading this book, or he could return one hundred years from now. Therefore, we need to keep watch for him. Furthermore, as we keep watch we need to be about the tasks he has assigned to us.

Are you a mother or a father? Then you need to fulfill your tasks well as you wait for the Lord Jesus to return to earth. Are you a businessperson? Then you need to do your job well as unto the Lord. Are you a son or daughter? You need to obey your parents. Are you a student? If so you need to do your very best in school and so please the Lord. When Jesus returns to earth, he doesn't want to find any of us loafing about. He wants to find us doing the things he has assigned for us to do.

THE SIXTH DAY OF CHRISTMAS

A third thing we can do to begin the year in a godly fashion is to **worship the Lord.** We read about Anna in Luke 2 that, "She never left the temple but worshiped night and day, fasting and praying."

Now we should not suppose that Anna literally slept in the Temple and spent every waking moment there. Luke is simply trying to make the point, in an exaggerated fashion, that Anna spent a lot of time worshiping the Lord in the Temple. The phrase is similar to one we have for people who are very active in the church. We say that they are at the church "whenever the doors are open."

Anna had a lot of time to spend at the Temple. She had been a widow most of her life. We are not told what she did to support herself financially. However, if she had a job outside her home, I'm sure she did it well. As a widow, Anna's extended family, or the Jewish community at large, may have supported her financially.

Not all of us have the same opportunities that Anna had. Some of us have more time than others that we can devote to worshiping the Lord on a daily basis. I don't believe the Lord wants us to give up our rightful responsibilities of parenting or earning a living just so we can worship him more often.

I think what the Lord does want those of us to do, who have less time on our hands, is he wants us to "practice his presence". That phrase, "The Practice of the Presence of God", comes from a 17th century Carmelite monk by the name of Nicholas Herman. This monk took the name Brother Lawrence, and as he was assigned to kitchen duty in his monastery, he had less time, perhaps, than the other monks, to apply himself to the devotional life. Therefore, Brother Lawrence tried to develop the habit of recognizing the presence of God in his everyday activities. It was said of Brother Lawrence, "That he was pleased when he could take up a straw from the ground for the love of God, seeking Him only, and nothing else, not even His gifts."

I believe God wants us all to become more like Brother Lawrence. I believe the Lord wants us to get into the habit of talking to him on a moment-by-moment basis. Get in the habit of lifting up quick prayers to the Lord all during the day. Talk to him when you get out of bed. Speak to him at meal times. Converse with him while you are driving in your car, but remember: you don't have to close your eyes! Talk to him while you are at work. Chat with him when you go to bed at night. Just carry on a running conversation with the Lord.

C. S. Lewis says, "We may ignore, but we can nowhere evade, the presence of God. The world is crowded with Him. He walks everywhere *incognito*." Lewis goes on to say that he has tried to make every pleasure a channel for adoration of God. "If I could always be what I aim at being, no pleasure would be too ordinary or too usual for such reception; from the first taste of the air when I look out of the window–one's whole cheek becomes a sort of palate–down to one's soft slippers at bed-time."[18]

Try it out and see if it doesn't help you to worship God throughout the day. Thank God for each little pleasure, then pause for just a moment to consider what kind of God we must serve who would give us the joy of so many little pleasures crowded into the everyday.

So much for how we can worship God everyday, but wouldn't it be good to follow Anna's example and set aside some *special* time to worship God as we each enter into this new year? You might take a day this week and fast. Skip a few meals just so that you can take the time while you would have been eating to focus on God. (And it isn't a bad plan after the binging of the holidays!) Set aside some special time to pray to God. Ask his forgiveness for the failings of the year past and ask him to help you begin the coming year with a fresh perspective on your life in him.

THE SEVENTH DAY OF CHRISTMAS

A final thing we can do to begin the year ahead in a godly fashion is to **witness.** We read about Anna that she "spoke about the child to all who were looking forward to the redemption of Jerusalem."

Do you spend time speaking about Jesus to others? If not, could it be because you have not spent enough time with Jesus himself? Could it be that you don't talk about him because you haven't really met him as Anna did?

Anna met the infant Savior in the temple and she could not conceal her delight. If we have truly met the Savior and if we are spending time worshiping him on a daily basis, then we will not be able to conceal our relationship with him.

Richard Halverson once wrote,

> For the New Testament Christians, witness was not a sales pitch.
>
> They simply shared, each in his own way, what they had received. Theirs was not a formally prepared, carefully worked-out presentation with a gimmick to manipulate conversation, and a 'closer' for an on-the-spot decision . . . but the spontaneous, irrepressible, effervescent enthusiasm of those who had met the most fascinating Person who ever lived...
>
> They had encountered Jesus Christ and it simply could not be concealed. They witnessed not because they had to, but because they could not help it.

If we have truly encountered Jesus Christ as Anna did then it should be evident to others. As Lloyd Ogilvie has said,

> The people around us can always read our hearts by our faces. The inner things we live with will always show up on our faces. The soul is dyed with the color of our commitment. Our task is not to argue, philosophize, speculate, cajole, but to live a life that demands an explanation. Is there anything about us that would force people to say, 'Now that's living! That's the way I wish I could live!' A joy-filled life will always demand an explanation—but too often we want Life without having to change our life-style.

Devotional Thoughts for the Holiday Season

Michael Green once defined evangelism simply as: overflow. Consider what would happen if you walked through life with a glass of water full to the brim. As you bumped into people along life's way, some of that water would overflow the rim of the glass and spill on to the people you meet. The same thing happens when Jesus fills us to overflowing; the Lord naturally spills out of our lives on to those we meet.

As we begin another year, some people are scared of what the future will bring. Others are riding high but finding that money cannot buy peace and contentment. Many have just celebrated Christmas but they do not know the joy of a personal relationship with the one whose birthday we celebrate. How are they to find comfort? How are they to find peace? How are they to discover the joy of a personal relationship with Jesus Christ? The only way they will discover Christ is if they see him in our lives and if we tell about him with our lips. We are the only Bible some people will ever read.

If you are like me, then you are probably not very good at doing any of these things. I'm not good at waiting. Often I am not watching for Christ to return; I would rather get on with my own plans. I do not always worship him on a daily basis. I am often too preoccupied with myself, and my problems. As a result, I often know no living Lord whom I can share with others. If you are like me then you may need to ask for the forgiveness of Christ for the times when you haven't done these things during the past year. Furthermore, we need to ask for the power of the Holy Spirit to do these things better as we enter into a new year. Why not talk to God right now and ask him for the forgiveness and the power that you need?

Ask him to fill you to overflowing with Jesus.

THE EIGHTH DAY OF CHRISTMAS

Mary Farwell writes: "I was listening to my 5-year-old son, Matthew, as he worked on his 'Speak and Spell' computer. He was concentrating intensely, typing words for the computer to say back to him.

"Matthew punched in the word 'God.' To his surprise, the computer said, 'Word not found.'

"He tried again with the same reply. With great disgust, he stared at the computer and told it in no uncertain terms, 'Jesus is not going to like this!'"

We can, from our human perspective, identify at least three types of people. There are those who have found a relationship with God and are seeking to know him better. There are those who are seeking God but have not yet found a relationship with him. Finally, there are those who, like the "Speak and Spell" computer, live their lives without any reference to God whatsoever.

Today, as we approach Epiphany, I would like to begin looking with you at eight signs of a seeker that we find in the account of the Magi who sought the newborn Christ child in Matthew 2:1-12,

> After Jesus was born in Bethlehem in Judea, during the time of King Herod, Magi from the east came to Jerusalem and asked, "Where is the one who has been born king of the Jews? We saw his star in the east and have come to worship him."
>
> When King Herod heard this he was disturbed, and all Jerusalem with him. When he had called together all the people's chief priests and teachers of the law, he asked them where the Christ was to be born. "In Bethlehem in Judea," they replied, "for this is what the prophet has written:
>
>> "'But you, Bethlehem, in the land of Judah,
>> are by no means least among the rulers of Judah;
>> for out of you will come a ruler

who will be the shepherd of my people Israel.'"

Then Herod called the Magi secretly and found out from them the exact time the star had appeared. He sent them to Bethlehem and said, "Go and make a careful search for the child. As soon as you find him, report to me, so that I too may go and worship him."

After they had heard the king, they went on their way, and the star they had seen in the east went ahead of them until it stopped over the place where the child was. When they saw the star, they were overjoyed. On coming to the house, they saw the child with his mother Mary, and they bowed down and worshiped him. Then they opened their treasures and presented him with gifts of gold and of incense and of myrrh. And having been warned in a dream not to go back to Herod, they returned to their country by another route.

I believe the first sign of a seeker after God is **hunger**. If you are a seeker, then you will have an all-consuming hunger for Christ.

In this passage, we see three different reactions to Jesus the King. First, there is the reaction of Herod who hated Christ. Herod did not want anyone else to be King of the Jews, so he hated any other potential king. Herod himself was not a legitimate heir to the Jewish throne because he was only a half-Jew. He had members of his own family killed if he thought that they might possibly take his throne away from him.

Now we think, "How horrible! What a despicable man!" However, isn't there a bit of Herod in each of us? We, like Herod, want to be on the throne. We want to be in control of our own lives and we tend to walk over anyone who gets in our way, even if that means walking over God.

The second reaction we see to Christ in this passage is that of the priests and scribes who were indifferent to the reality of the Messiah. The priests and scribes knew what the Hebrew Scriptures said about where the Messiah was to be born, but they had no interest in going to see him. They were apparently more interested in playing their own religious game than in actually meeting God.

The third reaction to Christ that we see in this passage is that of the Magi who hungered after Christ. These Magi were foreigners from the east. Originally, the Magi were Medes who tried to overthrow the Persians. They failed in their attempt and thereafter became priests. They in fact became teachers of the Persian kings. They were kingmakers, if you will, and perhaps that is where the story of there being three kings originated.

These Magi, or great men, may well have been from Babylon. It may be that they learned about the Messiah by reading the book of Daniel. For the Hebrew prophet Daniel had lived for a time in Babylon and had been a teacher of the Babylonian wise men. (Daniel 2:48) Or else these Magi may have learned about the Christ from the Jewish community that still existed in Babylon at the time of Christ's birth. We do not know with certainty how these Persian wise men found out about the Christ. However, one thing we do know, having heard of him, they hungered for him. Why else would they have embarked on such a long journey and asked everywhere they went, "Where is he who is born King of the Jews?"

In the Antarctic summer of 1908-9, Sir Ernest Shackleton and three companions attempted to travel to the South Pole from their winter quarters. They set off with four ponies to help carry the load. Weeks later, their ponies dead, rations all but exhausted, they turned back toward their base, their goal not accomplished. Altogether, they trekked 127 days.

On the return journey, as Shackleton records in *The Heart of the Antarctic*, the time was spent talking about food–elaborate feasts, gourmet delights, sumptuous menus. As they staggered along, suffering from dysentery, not knowing whether they would survive, every waking hour was occupied with thoughts of eating.

Jesus, who also knew the ravages of food deprivation during his adult life, said, "Blessed are those who hunger and thirst for righteousness." We can understand Shackleton's obsession with food, which offers a glimpse of the passion Jesus wants us to have for a relationship with him.

The Magi hungered after some kind of relationship with the Christ of whom they had read. Are we hungering after a relationship with Christ? If so, our hunger reveals the fact that we are seekers.

THE NINTH DAY OF CHRISTMAS

The second sign of a seeker after God that we see in Matthew 2:1-12 is a **miraculous journey.** If we are seeking after the one true God then our spiritual journey will be miraculous—a sovereign work of God. A star miraculously led the Magi to the place where the Christ child was living.

How gracious it was of God to guide the Magi in a way that they could understand. For you see, many people in that day, in the ancient east, believed in astrology. The Magi were apparently stargazers who tried to read various messages in the heavens. In fact, the Bible tells us that the stars do have a message for us. Psalm 19:1 says, "The heavens declare the glory of God; the skies proclaim the work of his hands." The heavens are constantly telling us of the reality of God. However, God, on this one occasion, chose to speak through the stars in a special way and guide the Magi by one particular star to where the Christ child was living. How gracious, and how miraculous of God to guide the Magi in this way.

Now you may think, "I wish God would speak to me like that and show me what he wants me to do with my life." Well, God does speak to us today. He speaks to us especially through the Scriptures and he supernaturally guides the circumstances of our lives, whether we realize it or not. Even when our circumstances seem the worst, that may be exactly where God is bringing about his special purpose for us.

John Yates writes,

> The only survivor of a shipwreck washed up on a small uninhabited island. He cried out to God to save him, and every day he scanned the horizon for help, but none seemed forthcoming.
>
> Exhausted, he eventually managed to build a rough hut and put his few possessions in it. But then one day, after hunting for food, he arrived home to find his little hut in flames, the smoke rolling up to the sky. The worst had happened; he was stung with grief.
>
> Early the next day, though, a ship drew near the island and rescued

him.

"How did you know I was here?" he asked the crew.

"We saw your smoke signal," they replied.

God may not be using a star to guide your life. In fact, you may feel, right now, as though God is totally absent from your life. However, your present difficulty may be the very instrument that God is using to bring about his best purpose for your life and the lives of others.

THE TENTH DAY OF CHRISTMAS

The third sign of a seeker that we find in Matthew 2:1-12 is **joy.** Joy will be overwhelmingly present in our lives if we are seeking after the one true God. We read that when the Magi saw the star they were overjoyed.

Roy Borges writes about Christmas in prison:

> Christmas night in confinement, alone in my cell, I read in my Bible about Paul and Silas, who were also inside a prison. Despite their miserable predicament, they were praying and singing hymns to God while the other prisoners listened.
>
> The lights went out and I stared at the ceiling from my bunk, wondering if I could praise God in the midst of my circumstances. I could hear a mouse nibbling on some crackers I left out for him. Then suddenly I heard a voice come out of the vent above the toilet. It was Andrew in the next cell. "Merry Christmas, Roy," he said.
>
> "Merry Christmas, Andrew," I replied.
>
> "Do you know any Christmas songs?" Andrew asked.
>
> "Yeah, I know a few."
>
> "I'll sing one if you'll sing one," he said.
>
> "What should we sing?"
>
> "Joy to the World." And he sang every verse. I sang the chorus with him. Then it was my turn and I chose "Silent Night." Then he sang "O Come All Ye Faithful," and I answered with "Feliz Navidad." …
>
> "I have another song," Andrew said, and sang "O Holy Night." Silence filled the quad as everyone listened. It was a moment I'll never forget. It not only reminded me of Paul and Silas, but it made me realize every day is Christmas when God has arrived. It wasn't just another day, and I wasn't alone. Emmanuel was in confinement with me, in my cell, blessing me.[19]

Open Before Christmas

The birth of Christ brings a joy that even the bleakest circumstances cannot completely extinguish in those who seek to know the Lord.

The fourth sign of a seeker is **knowledge**. When we find Christ, we will know him and not be deceived.

That was the case for the Magi. When they came to the house and saw the child with his mother Mary, they didn't then leave and go looking somewhere else for the Christ. They knew, supernaturally, that they had found the one they were looking for. They knew that they didn't need to search any longer. They knew because one look at this child satisfied all the spiritual hunger they had ever experienced. In his presence was fullness of joy.

In our day, it is popular to exalt doubt and to debunk certainty. We are like the family of mice who lived all their lives in a large piano. To them in their piano world came the music of the instrument, filling all the dark spaces with sound and harmony. At first, the mice were impressed by it. They drew comfort and wonder from the thought that there was someone who made the music—though invisible to them—above, yet close to them. They loved to think of the Great Player whom they could not see.

Then one day a daring mouse climbed up part of the piano and returned very thoughtful. He had found out how music was made. Wires were the secret; tightly stretched wires of graduated lengths that trembled and vibrated. They must revise all their old beliefs: none but the most conservative mouse could any longer believe in the Unseen Player.

Later, another explorer carried the explanation further. Hammers were now the secret, numbers of hammers dancing and leaping on the wires. This was a more complicated theory, but it all went to show that they lived in a purely mechanical and mathematical world. The Unseen Player came to be thought of as a myth. However, the pianist continued to play.[20]

How would it be if one of the mice should crawl out of the piano and meet the piano player? Well then, the mouse that crawled out would certainly know he had seen the piano player and he would not be deceived.

On the other hand, how would it be if the piano player were to crawl into the piano? Certainly, he would frighten the mice by his mere size and they would run in fear. Thus, if the pianist wanted to have a relationship with the mice he would have to become small like them. In fact, he would have to become a mouse. How then would the mice react to one mouse among them who claimed to be the pianist? Some might recognize in this mouse something beyond the merely mouse-like in nature. Those same mice might even bow down and worship this piano-player-become-mouse, just as the Magi worshiped Christ. Other mice might execute this piano-player-pretender as a crazy mouse, just as Christ was crucified upon a cross. However, the sign of a true seeker-mouse would be that he would recognize the piano player when he met him.

Christians are not being narrow-minded when they say that Jesus is the Christ and that he is the only way to God. They are simply recognizing the piano player when they see him and repeating the claims of the piano player himself. That is the sign of a true seeker.

THE ELEVENTH DAY OF CHRISTMAS

The fifth sign of a true seeker is **courageous confession**. If we are truly seeking after God, then we will make a clear, courageous confession of truth. The Magi made a clear, courageous confession of truth when they told everyone in Jerusalem that they had come to worship the one who had been born the king of the Jews.

Again, we see three responses to Jesus the King. Herod told the Magi that he wanted to go and worship the Christ child too. However, this was a false confession. Herod only wanted to know where the Christ child was so that he could eliminate him.

Many others in Jerusalem at that time were probably afraid to openly confess faith in Jesus the child-king. They were afraid of what Herod would do to them if they confessed their allegiance to this new king, this usurper of Herod's throne.

Then there was the response of the Magi. They were oblivious, at first, to all of Herod's machinations. All they cared about was finding the King. Thus, they told everyone about their search. Clear, courageous confession of truth is the sign of a true seeker.

In *Living Above the Level of Mediocrity*, Chuck Swindoll writes:

> On Sunday, believers arrived at a house church in the Soviet Union in small groups throughout the day so as not to arouse the suspicion of KGB informers. They began by singing a hymn quietly. Suddenly, in walked two soldiers with loaded weapons at the ready. One shouted, 'If you wish to renounce your commitment to Jesus Christ, leave now!'
>
> Two or three quickly left, then another. After a few more seconds, two more.
>
> 'This is your last chance. Either turn against your faith in Christ,' he ordered, 'or stay and suffer the consequences.'
>
> Two more slipped out into the night. No one else moved. Parents

with children trembling beside them looked down reassuringly, fully expecting to be gunned down or imprisoned.

The other soldier closed the door, looked back at those who stood against the wall and said, 'Keep your hands up–but this time in praise to our Lord Jesus Christ. We, too, are Christians. We were sent to another house church several weeks ago to arrest a group of believers . . .'

The other soldier interrupted, 'But, instead, we were converted! We have learned by experience, however, that unless people are willing to die for their faith, they cannot be fully trusted.'

The believers that remained in that house church, fully expecting to be executed or imprisoned, were making a clear, courageous confession of truth, albeit a silent confession. What about us? How might we fare in the same circumstances? How do we live now? Are we clearly and courageously confessing faith in Christ? If we have been presented with the evidence of the claims of Christ and we are still sitting on the sidelines, perhaps it is time to make a decision and get in the game.

THE TWELFTH DAY OF CHRISTMAS

The sixth sign of a true seeker is **Christ-centered worship**. We read that upon seeing the Christ the Magi bowed down and worshiped him.

Today in Bethlehem on the site of Jesus' supposed birthplace there stands The Church of the Nativity. It is an interesting fact that to get into the Church of the Nativity you must enter through a small door that forces you to bow down. This reminds us that the only safe way to approach Jesus is on our knees.

In *Touch and Live,* George Vandeman writes:

"A young stranger to the Alps was making his first climb, accompanied by two stalwart guides. It was a steep, hazardous ascent. But he felt secure with one guide ahead and one following. For hours they climbed. And now, breathless, they reached for those rocks protruding through the snow above them–the summit.

"The guide ahead wished to let the stranger have the first glorious view of heaven and earth, and moved aside to let him go first. Forgetting the gales that would blow across those summit rocks, the young man leaped to his feet. But the chief guide dragged him down. 'On your knees, sir!' he shouted. 'You are never safe here except on your knees.'"

In the same way, we are never safe in the presence of Almighty God, even the God-Man Jesus, unless we approach him on our knees. The Magi must have sensed this, so they bowed down and worshiped the Christ.

The seventh sign of a true seeker is **giving**. If we are true seekers then we will give Christ what he is worth.

The Magi gave to the young Jesus: gold, frankincense and myrrh. Gold is a gift for a king. Matthew tells us Jesus is the great King, the Son of David. Jesus wants to be king in our lives today.

Frankincense is for a priest. Jesus is our great high priest who has offered the sacrifice of his own body upon the cross for our sins.

Finally, myrrh is an appropriate gift for one who is going to die, for it is an embalming spice. Jesus was born to die upon the cross for sinners like you and me.

Devotional Thoughts for the Holiday Season

The Magi gave to Christ what he was worthy of. That's what worship is all about, giving Christ what he is worth. Being a Christian means giving as much as we know of ourselves to as much as we know of Christ.

That's what Christ is worthy of. He is worthy to receive our hearts and our lives.

EPIPHANY

The final sign of a seeker that we see in Matthew 2:1-12 is **protection**. The Magi were warned in a dream not to go back to Herod. Thus, they returned home by another route. God was protecting them because of their clear, courageous confession of the truth.

When my father became a Christian and left his work in organized crime, some of the gangsters he had been working for came calling on him. My dad explained to them that his life was under new management, then the gangsters turned and walked away. That was an unexplainable phenomenon by the standards of this world, but it is explainable in God's reckoning. For my dad had claimed the verse, "When a man's ways please the Lord, he makes even his enemies to be at peace with him."

Some weeks later, my father was speaking to a group of Christian businesspeople in Hollywood, California. He told the story of his conversion at the Billy Graham meeting, how he had quit organized crime, and his decision not to go to Missouri on November 10, 1949 to set up the electronic system of past-post betting for St. Louis Andy.

After my father's talk, a woman who worked in the Mayor's office stood up and said:

> Mr. Vaus doesn't know me, but I thought he would be interested in hearing about a report that came to our office. The FBI informed us that if Mr. Vaus had travelled to St. Louis on November 10, he wouldn't have lived more than thirty minutes after arrival because there was a rival gang set up to kill him.

If we make a clear, courageous confession of faith in Christ we can be sure that God will protect us. Furthermore, even if we must make the ultimate sacrifice, which few of us are called to make, of giving up our life-blood for what we believe, then won't the sacrifice be worth it? Won't it be worth it to gain heaven, rather than to deny Christ?

So there, you have them, the eight signs of a seeker. However, there is a problem. The Apostle Paul tells us that there is "no one who seeks God."

(Romans 3:11) In and of ourselves, none of us ever seek after God. C. S. Lewis says that if we did, it would be like the mouse seeking after the cat.

A little boy wrote a letter to Santa that went like this: "Dear Santa, there are three little boys who live at our house. There is Jeffrey; he is two. There is David; he is four, and there is Norman; he is seven. Jeffrey is good some of the time. David is good some of the time ... but Norman is good all of the time. I am Norman."

We aren't Normans, are we? We aren't good. We don't seek after God. If we are ever going to seek after God, he must first seek after us. He must first come into our lives and change our hearts by the Holy Spirit. Why not pray, right now, and ask God to change you so that you will seek after him every day?

CONCLUSION

A repeated refrain we have heard during our journey through Advent and The Twelve Days of Christmas is that we cannot truly separate Christmas and the cross, Incarnation and Redemption, the birth of Jesus and the sacrifice of Christ, without missing important aspects of the truth. That is one of the great values of celebrating all the great fasts and feasts of the Church Year: it helps us to see the entire story of salvation in context, in all of its integrity. I hope that reading this book has been for you either the beginning of a deeper appreciation of the riches of celebrating the Church Year, or at least an effective help along the way to that end.

As I shared in the Introduction, the celebration of Advent goes back to at least the fourth century. However, Easter has been celebrated since the first century. Lent, the season in the Church Year that leads up to Easter, commemorates Jesus' forty days of temptation and privation in the wilderness. The rest of the Church Year, much of it devoted to what is called "Ordinary Time" pivots around these two great holidays of Christmas and Easter.

I can certainly relate to those who find Christian worship structured according to these seasons to be rather mysterious. For my own part, I have spent much of my Christian life within a church tradition that has not celebrated all the great fasts and feasts of the Church. However, I find the more I grow as a Christian, the more I want to learn about the treasures of Christian wisdom that can be mined from the writings and practices of Christians through the centuries. One of those treasures is the celebration of the rhythm of the Church Year.

One tool that has helped me to discover the riches of this rhythm is the Book of Common Prayer of the Anglican tradition. Using the services of Morning and Evening Prayer as a guide to my private devotional life has helped me to discover the joy of living within the rhythm of the liturgy of the Church. As depicted in the following illustration, many of the days of our lives are lived in "Ordinary Time".

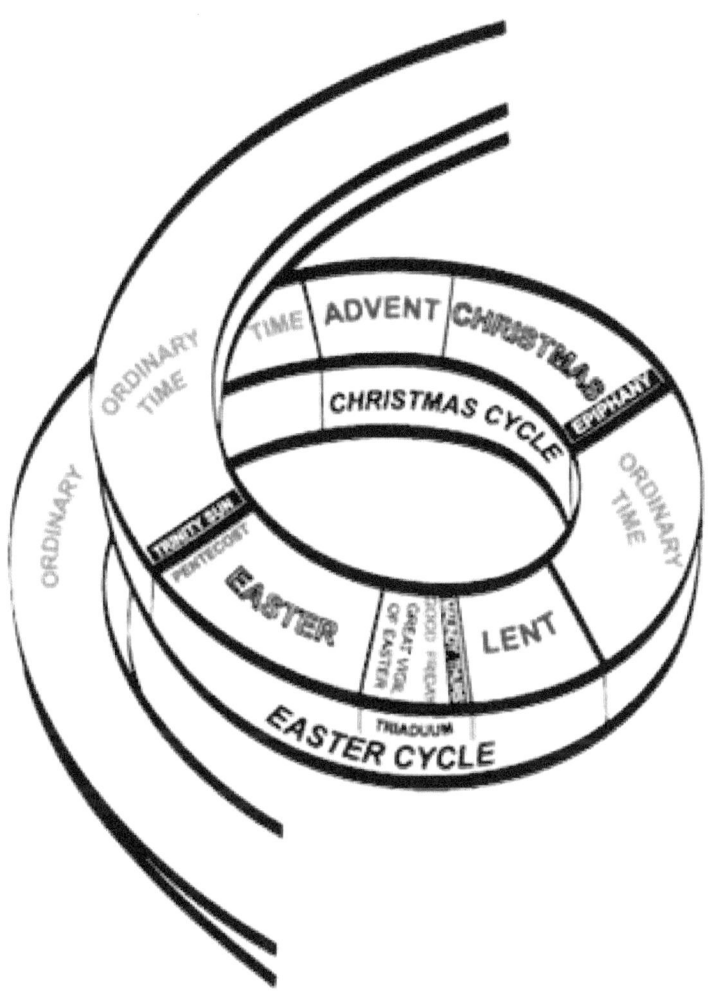

However, living within the rhythm of the Church Year has made many of those days more extra-ordinary for me. It relates my sometimes seemingly meaningless life to a larger pattern of purpose. Utilizing the Book of Common Prayer for my daily devotions has enabled me to better orient my life vertically, in daily worship of our Triune God, but also horizontally, it has connected me to the communion of saints down through the ages.

Thus, I commend The Book of Common Prayer to you. It is just one resource, from one church tradition, that helps connect us to the larger communion of saints beyond our particular time and place. There are many other resources out there as well. Whatever resources you choose to assist your journey through the Church Year from this point on, I pray that the Lord of the Church, the Sovereign God of all traditions, will be with you, as you journey further up and further in.

Allow me to close with the words of one of my favorite writers on the spiritual life, Henri Nouwen:

> The beginning of the spiritual life is often difficult not only because the powers which cause us to worry are so strong but also because the presence of God's Spirit seems barely noticeable. If, however, we are faithful to our disciplines, a new hunger will make itself known. This new hunger is the first sign of God's presence. When we remain attentive to this divine presence, we will be led always deeper into the kingdom. There, to our joyful surprise, we will discover that all things are being made new. [21]

END NOTES

1 Lewis, C. S., *Reflections on the Psalms*, London: Geoffrey Bles, 1958, pp. 48-49.
2 http://www.newadvent.org/cathen/01165a.htm
3 http://cptryon.org/prayer/adx/adwreath.html
4 http://www.cresourcei.org/cyadvent.html
5 http://www.newadvent.org/cathen/03724b.htm
6 Ellen Cowan, Rome, GA., "Lite Fare", *Christian Reader*.
7 Ravi Zacharias, *Deliver Us From Evil*.
8 Lewis, C. S., *Miracles*, London: Geoffrey Bles, 1947, p. 135.
9 Tewell, Thomas K., Preaching Today.
10 The statue of the child Jesus holding the world is the Infant Jesus of Prague. The National Shrine for the Holy Infant of Prague is located in New Haven, Connecticut. There is substantial worldwide Catholic devotion to the child Jesus represented by the statue of him holding a globe in one hand and blessing with his other.
11 Gene Weingarten, "Pearls before Breakfast," The Washington Post (4-10-07); submitted to PreachingToday.com by Stephen Nordbye, Charlton, Massachusetts.
12 Bruce Thieleman
13 Illustration taken from a sermon by the Reverend Peter Marshall, Sr.
14 Lewis, C. S., *Miracles*, pp. 56-57.
15 Ibid. p. 166.
16 Hooper, Walter, editor, The Collected Letters of C. S. Lewis, Volume II, New York: HarperCollins, 2004, p. 595.
17 Lewis, C. S., *Mere Christianity*, Book IV, chapter 5, paragraphs 3-5.
18 Lewis, C. S., *Letters to Malcolm: Chiefly on Prayer*.
19 Roy Borges, "O Holy Night," Today's Christian (November/December 2006), p. 66.
20 This story originally appeared in *The London Observer*.
21 Henri J.M. Nouwen, *Making All Things New: An Invitation to the Spiritual Life*, New York: HarperCollins, 1981.

WILL VAUS

- was born outside of New York City and grew up in Southern California.
- is the son of Jim Vaus, former organized crime wiretapper who came to Christ through the ministry of Billy Graham in 1949.
- holds a Bachelor of Arts degree in drama from the University of California at San Diego and a Master of Divinity degree from Princeton Theological Seminary.
- has served as a pastor in California, South Carolina and Pennsylvania.
- is the president of Will Vaus Ministries, through which he has communicated the love of Christ around the world since 1988.
- is the author of *Mere Theology: A Guide to the Thought of C. S. Lewis*, *My Father Was a Gangster: The Jim Vaus Story*, *The Professor of Narnia: The C. S. Lewis Story*, *Speaking of Jack: A C. S. Lewis Discussion Guide*, *The Hidden Story of Narnia: A Book-by-Book Guide to Lewis' Spiritual Themes* and *Keys To Growth: Meditations on the Acts of the Apostles*.
- and his wife, Becky, have been married since 1988 and have three sons: James, Jonathan and Joshua.
- has a website you can visit: www.willvaus.com

Other Books of Interest

C. S. Lewis

C. S. Lewis: Views From Wake Forest - Essays on C. S. Lewis
Michael Travers, editor

Contains sixteen scholarly presentations from the international C. S. Lewis convention in Wake Forest, NC. Walter Hooper shares his important essay "Editing C. S. Lewis," a chronicle of publishing decisions after Lewis' death in 1963.

"*Scholars from a variety of disciplines address a wide range of issues. The happy result is a fresh and expansive view of an author who well deserves this kind of thoughtful attention.*"
    Diana Pavlac Glyer, author of *The Company They Keep*

The Hidden Story of Narnia:
A Book-By-Book Guide to Lewis' Spiritual Themes
Will Vaus

A book of insightful commentary equally suited for teens or adults – Will Vaus points out connections between the *Narnia* books and spiritual/biblical themes, as well as between ideas in the *Narnia* books and C. S. Lewis' other books. Learn what Lewis himself said about the overarching and unifying thematic structure of the Narnia books. That is what this book explores; what C. S. Lewis called "the hidden story" of Narnia. Each chapter includes questions for individual use or small group discussion.

Why I Believe in Narnia:
33 Reviews and Essays on the Life and Work of C. S. Lewis
James Como

Chapters range from reviews of critical books, documentaries and movies to evaluations of Lewis' books to biographical analysis.

"*A valuable, wide-ranging collection of essays by one of the best informed and most acute commentators on Lewis' work and ideas.*"
    Peter Schakel, author of *Imagination & the Arts in C. S. Lewis*

C. S. Lewis Goes to Heaven: A Reader's Guide to The Great Divorce
David G. Clark

This is the first book devoted solely to this often neglected book and the first to reveal several important secrets Lewis concealed within the story. Lewis felt his imaginary trip to Hell and Heaven was far better than his book *The Screwtape Letters*, which has become a classic. Clark is an ordained minister who has taught courses on Lewis for more than 30 years and is a New Testament and Greek scholar with a Doctor of Philosophy degree in Biblical Studies from the University of Notre Dame. Readers will discover the many literary and biblical influences Lewis utilized in writing his brilliant novel.

C. S. Lewis & Philosophy as a Way of Life
Adam Barkman

C. S. Lewis is rarely thought of as a "philosopher" per se despite having both studied and taught philosophy for several years at Oxford. Lewis's long journey to Christianity was essentially philosophical – passing through seven different stages. This 624 page book is an invaluable reference for C. S. Lewis scholars and fans alike

C. S. Lewis: His Literary Achievement
Colin Manlove

"This is a positively brilliant book, written with splendor, elegance, profundity and evidencing an enormous amount of learning. This is probably not a book to give a first-time reader of Lewis. But for those who are more broadly read in the Lewis corpus this book is an absolute gold mine of information. The author gives us a magnificent overview of Lewis' many writings, tracing for us thoughts and ideas which recur throughout, and at the same time telling us how each book differs from the others. I think it is not extravagant to call C. S. Lewis: His Literary Achievement a tour de force."
Robert Merchant, *St. Austin Review*, Book Review Editor

Mythopoeic Narnia:
Memory, Metaphor, and Metamorphoses in The Chronicles of Narnia
Salwa Khoddam

Dr. Khoddam, the founder of the C. S. Lewis and Inklings Society (2004), has been teaching university courses using Lewis' books for over 25 years. Her book offers a fresh approach to the Narnia books based on an inquiry into Lewis' readings and use of classical and Christian symbols. She explores the literary and intellectual contexts of these stories, the traditional myths and motifs, and places them in the company of the greatest Christian mythopoeic works of Western literature. In Lewis' imagination, memory and metaphor interact to advance his purpose – a Christian metamorphosis. *Mythopoeic Narnia* helps to open the door for readers into the magical world of the Western imagination.

Speaking of Jack: A C. S. Lewis Discussion Guide
Will Vaus

C. S. Lewis societies have been forming around the world since the first one started in New York City in 1969. Will Vaus has started and led three groups himself. *Speaking of Jack* is the result of Vaus' experience in leading those Lewis societies. Included here are introductions to most of Lewis' books as well as questions designed to stimulate discussion about Lewis' life and work. These materials have been "road-tested" with real groups made up of young and old, some very familiar with Lewis and some newcomers. *Speaking of Jack* may be used in an existing book discussion group, to start a C. S. Lewis society, or to guide your own exploration of Lewis' books.

George MacDonald

Diary of an Old Soul & The White Page Poems
George MacDonald and Betty Aberlin

The first edition of George MacDonald's book of daily poems included a blank page opposite each page of poems. Readers were invited to write their own reflections on the "white page." MacDonald wrote: "Let your white page be ground, my print be seed, growing to golden ears, that faith and hope may feed." Betty Aberlin responded to MacDonald's invitation with daily poems of her own.

"Betty Aberlin's close readings of George MacDonald's verses and her thoughtful responses to them speak clearly of her poetic gifts and spiritual intelligence."
   Luci Shaw, poet

George MacDonald: Literary Heritage and Heirs
Roderick McGillis, editor

This latest collection of 14 essays sets a new standard that will influence MacDonald studies for many more years. George MacDonald experts are increasingly evaluating his entire corpus within the nineteenth century context.

"This comprehensive collection represents the best of contemporary scholarship on George MacDonald."
   Rolland Hein, author of *George MacDonald: Victorian Mythmaker*

In the Near Loss of Everything: George MacDonald's Son in America
Dale Wayne Slusser

In the summer of 1887, George MacDonald's son Ronald, newly engaged to artist Louise Blandy, sailed from England to America to teach school. The next summer he returned to England to marry Louise and bring her back to America. On August 27, 1890, Louise died, leaving him with an infant daughter. Ronald once described losing a beloved spouse as "the near loss of everything". Dale Wayne Slusser unfolds this poignant story with unpublished letters and photos that give readers a glimpse into the close-knit MacDonald family.

A Novel Pulpit: Sermons From George MacDonald's Fiction
David L. Neuhouser

"In MacDonald's novels, the Christian teaching emerges out of the characters and story line, the narrator's comments, and inclusion of sermons given by the fictional preachers. The sermons in the novels are shorter than the ones in collections of MacDonald's sermons and so are perhaps more accessible for some. In any case, they are both stimulating and thought-provoking. This collection of sermons from ten novels serve to bring out the 'freshness and brilliance' of MacDonald's message."
   From the author's introduction

Through the Year with George MacDonald: 366 Daily Readings
Rolland Hein, editor

These page-length excerpts from sermons, novels and letters are given an appropriate theme/heading and a complementary Scripture passage for daily reading. An inspiring introduction to the artistic soul and Christian vision of George MacDonald.

Behind the Back of the North Wind:
Critical Essays on George MacDonald's Classic Children's Book
John Pennington and Roderick McGillis, editors

The unique blend of fairy tale atmosphere and social realism in this novel laid the groundwork for modern fantasy literature. Sixteen essays by various authors are accompanied by an instructive introduction, extensive index, and beautiful illustrations.

Shadows and Chivalry:
C. S. Lewis and George MacDonald on Suffering, Evil, and Death
Jeff McInnis

Shadows and Chivalry studies the influence of George MacDonald, a nineteenth-century Scottish novelist and fantasy writer, upon one of the most influential writers of modern times, C. S. Lewis – the creator of Narnia, literary critic, and best-selling apologist. This study attempts to trace the overall affect of MacDonald's work on Lewis's thought and imagination. Without ever ceasing to be a story of one man's influence upon another, the study also serves as an exploration of each writer's thought on, and literary visions of, good and evil.

Christian Living

The Living Word of the Living God:
A Beginner's Guide to Reading and Understanding the Bible
Rev. Tom Furrer

This book is based on over 20 years experience of teaching the Bible to confirmation classes at Episcopal churches in Connecticut. Chapters from Genesis to Revelation.

Keys to Growth: Meditations on the Acts of the Apostles
Will Vaus

Every living things or person requires certain ingredients in order to grow, and if a thing or person is not growing, it is dying. *The Acts of the Apostles* is a book that is all about growth. Will Vaus has been meditating and preaching on *Acts* for the past 30 years. In this volume, he offers the reader forty-one keys from the entire book of Acts to unlock spiritual growth in everyday life.

Called to Serve: Life as a Firefighter-Deacon
Deacon Anthony R. Surozenski

Called to Serve is the story of one man's dream to be a firefighter. But dreams have a way of taking detours – so Tony Surozenski became a teacher and eventually a volunteer firefighter. And when God enters the picture, Tony is faced with a choice. Will he give up firefighting to follow another call? After many years, Tony's two callings are finally united – in service as a fire chaplain at Ground Zero after the 9-11 attacks and in other ways he could not have imagined. Tony is Chief Chaplain's aid for the Massachusetts Corp of Fire Chaplains and Director for the Office of the Diaconate of the Diocese of Worchester, Massachusetts.

Harry Potter

The Order of Harry Potter: The Literary Skill of the Hogwarts Epic
Colin Manlove

Colin Manlove, a popular conference speaker and author of over a dozen books, has earned an international reputation as an expert on fantasy and children's literature. His book, *From Alice to Harry Potter*, is a survey of 400 English fantasy books. In *The Order of Harry Potter*, he compares and contrasts *Harry Potter* with works by "Inklings" writers J.R.R. Tolkien, C.S. Lewis and Charles Williams; he also examines Rowling's treatment of the topic of imagination; her skill in organization and the use of language; and the book's underlying motifs and themes.

Harry Potter & Imagination: The Way Between Two Worlds
Travis Prinzi

Imaginative literature places a reader between two worlds: the story world and the world of daily life, and challenges the reader to imagine and to act for a better world. Starting with discussion of Harry Potter's more important themes, *Harry Potter & Imagination* takes readers on a journey through the transformative power of those themes for both the individual and for culture by placing Rowling's series in its literary, historical, and cultural contexts.

Repotting Harry Potter: A Professor's Guide for the Serious Re-Reader
Rowling Revisited: Return Trips to Harry, Fantastic Beasts, Quidditch, & Beedle the Bard
James W. Thomas

In *Repotting Harry Potter* and his sequel book *Rowling Revisited*, Dr. James W. Thomas points out the humor, puns, foreshadowing and literary parallels in the Potter books. In *Rowling Revisited*, readers will especially find useful three extensive appendixes – "Fantastic Beasts and the Pages Where You'll Find Them," "Quidditch Through the Pages," and "The Books in the Potter Books." Dr. Thomas makes re-reading the Potter books even more rewarding and enjoyable.

The Deathly Hallows Lectures:
The Hogwarts Professor Explains Harry's Final Adventure
John Granger

In *The Deathly Hallows Lectures,* John Granger reveals the finale's brilliant details, themes, and meanings. *Harry Potter* fans will be surprised by and delighted with Granger's explanations of the three dimensions of meaning in *Deathly Hallows*. Ms. Rowling has said that alchemy sets the "parameters of magic" in the series; after reading the chapter-length explanation of *Deathly Hallows* as the final stage of the alchemical Great Work, the serious reader will understand how important literary alchemy is in understanding Rowling's artistry and accomplishment.

Sociology and Harry Potter: 22 Enchanting Essays on the Wizarding World
Jenn Simms, editor

Modeled on an Introduction to Sociology textbook. this books is not simply about the series, but also used the series to facilitate reader's understanding of the discipline of sociology and a development of a sociological approach to viewing social reality. It is a case of high quality academic scholarship written in a form and on a topic accessible to non-academics. As such, it is written to appeal to Harry Potter fans and the general reading public. Contributors include professional sociologists from eight countries.

Harry Potter, Still Recruiting:
An Inner Look at Harry Potter Fandom
Valerie Frankel, editor

The Harry Potter phenomenon has created a new world: one of Quidditch in the park, lightning earrings, endless parodies, a new genre of music, and fan conferences of epic proportions. This book attempts to document everything - exploring costuming, crafting, gaming, and more, with essays and interviews straight from the multitude of creators. From children to adults, fans are delighting the world with an explosion of captivating activities and experiences, all based on Rowling's delightful series.

Hog's Head Conversations: Essays on Harry Potter
Travis Prinzi, editor

Ten fascinating essays on Harry Potter are divided into five sections: Conversations on 1) Literary Value, 2) Eternal Truth, 3) Imagination, 4) Literary Criticism, and 5) Characters. Contributors include the following popular Potter writers and speakers: John Granger, James W. Thomas, Colin Manlove, and Travis Prinzi.

Fiction

The Iona Conspiracy (from The Remnant Chronicles book series)
Gary Gregg

Readers find themselves on a modern adventure through ancient Celtic myth and legend as thirteen year old Jacob uncovers his destiny within "the remnant" of the Sporrai Order. As the Iona Academy comes under the control of educational reformers and ideological scientists, Jacob finds himself on a dangerous mission to the sacred Scottish island of Iona and discovers how his life is wrapped up with the fate of the long lost cover of *The Book of Kells*. From its connections to Arthurian legend to references to real-life people, places, and historical mysteries, *Iona* is an adventure that speaks to eternal truths as well as the challenges of the modern world. A young adult novel, *Iona* can be enjoyed by the entire family.

Poets and Poetry

Remembering Roy Campbell: The Memoirs of his Daughters, Anna and Tess
Introduction by Judith Lütge Coullie, editor
Preface by Joseph Pearce

Anna and Teresa Campbell were the daughters of the handsome young South African poet and writer, Roy Campbell (1901-1957), and his beautiful English wife, Mary Garman. In their frank and moving memoirs, Anna and Tess recall the extraordinary, and often very difficult, lives they shared with their exceptional parents. The book includes over 50 photos, 344 footnotes, a timeline of Campbell's life, and a complete index.

In the Eye of the Beholder: How to See the World Like a Romantic Poet
Louis Markos

Born out of the French Revolution and its radical faith that a nation could be shaped and altered by the dreams and visions of its people, British Romantic Poetry was founded on a belief that the objects and realities of our world, whether natural or human, are not fixed in stone but can be molded and transformed by the visionary eye of the poet. Unlike many of the books written on Romanticism, which devote many pages to the poets and few pages to their poetry, the focus here is firmly on the poems themselves. The author thereby draws the reader intimately into the life of these poems. A separate bibliographical essay is provided for readers listing accessible biographies of each poet and critical studies of their work.

The Cat on the Catamaran: A Christmas Tale
John Martin

Here is a modern-day parable of a modern-day cat with modern-day attitudes. Riverboat Dan is a "cool" cat on a perpetual vacation from responsibility. He's *The Cat on the Catamaran* – sailing down the river of life. Dan keeps his guilty conscience from interfering with his fun until he runs into trouble. But will he have the courage to believe that it's never too late to change course? (For ages 10 to adult)

"*This book is a joy, and as companionable as a good-natured cat.*"
Walter Hooper, author of *C. S. Lewis: Companion and Guide*

The Half Blood Poems
Inspired by the Stories of J.K. Rowling
Christine Lowther

Like Harry Potter, Christine's poetry can soar above the tragic to discover the heroic and beautiful in such poems as "Neville, Unlikely Rebel", "For Our Wide-Armed Mothers," and "A Boy's Hands." There are 71 poems divided into seven chapters that correspond to the seven books. Fans of Harry Potter will experience once again many of the emotions they felt reading the books – emotions presented most effectively through a poet's words.

Pop Culture

To Love Another Person: A Spiritual Journey Through Les Miserables
John Morrison

The powerful story of Jean Valjean's redemption is beloved by readers and theatergoers everywhere. In this companion and guide to Victor Hugo's masterpiece, author John Morrison unfolds the spiritual depth and breadth of this classic novel and broadway musical.

Through Common Things: Philosophical Reflections on Popular Culture
Adam Barkman

"*Barkman presents us with an amazingly wide-ranging collection of philosophical reflections grounded in the everyday things of popular culture – past and present, eastern and western, factual and fictional. Throughout his encounters with often surprising subject-matter (the value of darkness?), he writes clearly and concisely, moving seamlessly between Aristotle and anime, Lord Buddha and Lord Voldemort.... This is an informative and entertaining book to read!*"
　　　　　Doug Bloomberg, Professor of Philosophy, Institute for Christian Studies

Above All Things: Essays on Christian Ethics and Popular Culture
Adam Barkman

"*Whether discussing Winnie the Pooh or The Walking Dead, this book digs up buried philosophical treasure. Those who don't normally think of themselves as philosophically inclined will be surprised and delighted as Barkman rescues philosophy from dry classroom abstractions and reveals how it fills the glorious messiness of everyday life.*"
　　　　　Dr. Kevin Flatt, Assistant Professor of History, Redeemer University College

Spotlight:
A Close-up Look at the Artistry and Meaning of Stephenie Meyer's Twilight Novels
John Granger

Stephenie Meyer's *Twilight* saga has taken the world by storm. But is there more to *Twilight* than a love story for teen girls crossed with a cheesy vampire-werewolf drama? *Spotlight* reveals the literary backdrop, themes, artistry, and meaning of the four Bella Swan adventures. *Spotlight* is the perfect gift for serious *Twilight* readers.

Virtuous Worlds: The Video Gamer's Guide to Spiritual Truth
John Stanifer

Popular titles like *Halo 3* and *The Legend of Zelda: Twilight Princess* fly off shelves at a mind-blowing rate. John Stanifer, an avid gamer, shows readers specific parallels between Christian faith and the content of their favorite games. Written with wry humor (including a heckler who frequently pokes fun at the author) this book will appeal to gamers and non-gamers alike. Those unfamiliar with video games may be pleasantly surprised to find that many elements in those "virtual worlds" also qualify them as "virtuous worlds."

www.ingramcontent.com/pod-product-compliance
Lightning Source LLC
Chambersburg PA
CBHW060456080526
44584CB00015B/1447